God's Hand in Brexit

A Prayer Handbook

Y. O. CEDAR

authorHOUSE®

AuthorHouse™ UK
1663 Liberty Drive
Bloomington, IN 47403 USA
www.authorhouse.co.uk
Phone: 0800.197.4150

Scripture quotations marked AMP are from The Amplified Bible, Old Testament copyright © 1965, 1987 by the Zondervan Corporation. The Amplified Bible, New Testament copyright © 1954, 1958, 1987 by The Lockman Foundation. Used by permission. All rights reserved.

Published by AuthorHouse 04/04/2017

ISBN: 978-1-5246-6411-4 (sc)
ISBN: 978-1-5246-6412-1 (e)

Print information available on the last page.

This book is printed on acid-free paper.

This book is dedicated to the Britain Prayer Court Family. Your dedication to prayer, faithfulness, friendship, and support helped launch me into my calling as an Intercessor.

Thank you so much, Pastor Rod and Julie Anderson, Dr Sharon Stone, and Elder Dikko for your love, support, training, mentoring, and impartation over the years, which helped me come to a greater understanding of who I am as an Ambassador for the Lord's Kingdom.

ACKNOWLEDGEMENTS

Father God thank you for assigning me to write this book. I couldn't have done it without your grace, wisdom, creativity and favour. Even the book is a work of your own Art. (The picture of the rainbow on the book cover was taken while we were praying).

I'm so grateful for my two beautiful children Kacey and Joshua who inspire and sharpen me every day. Being Mum to you has been very instrumental in my walk with the lord.

A massive thank you to each intercessor who co-laboured with me in prayer during the 40 days at Parliament Square. (I'd love to name you all here but you have chosen to be unknown). I treasure you and very honoured to co-labour with you in advancing the lords kingdom.

Elder Abi Dikko thank you for believing in me and for being a mother to me when I most needed one.

I acknowledge Pastor Nims and Edosa Obunge of Freedoms Ark Church for the foundation that you gave me during the first twelve years of my born-again experience and for planting the seed of the governmental anointing in me.

I recognise the wisdom of the Lord in planting me in a praying church at CCF (Commonwealth Community Church) since 2011. Pastor Rod and Julie Anderson your rich teachings on prayer and intercession have been so instrumental in my awakening to the call to intercession.

Thank you, Dr Sharon Stone for believing in me, for the mentoring, support and apostolic-prophetic training that has impacted me so greatly.

I thank Sean Feutch for introducing me to David's Tent Burn. The David's Tent worship meetings awakened me to a greater intimacy with Father God. I'm also deeply blessed by Jesus Culture and Bethel Ministries for the new sound of Worship and the SOZO's that brought freedom and liberty to me at a deeper level.

A big thank you to all who gave advice and feedback on the book development. Especially Juney Kelson, Dr Jennifer, Margaret Kassam, Lady Carol Baker, Ian Boston, Elder Abi Dikko, Bola Fadahunsi and Udoka Ohuonu.

Deedee Winter – In a very short space of time you have impacted me greatly.

And a big thank you to all Britain Prayer Court Intercessors especially those who contributed at the EU Prayer Summit.

CONTENTS

FOREWORD

The power of prayer keeps the soul in authentic intimacy with God, bringing supernatural help, just when we need it, and giving us the desires of our hearts. Maturity comes with responsibility and we will grow as we pray for our families and nation, trusting the future to be flooded by God's goodness. Our life assignments may begin with 'breakthrough' praying, but end up with what I call 'governance' praying. As Christians, we must never grow faint and weary, but keep on praying. This book will encourage you and open your heart in fresh ways to boldly decree God's goodness.

On September 15, 1983, I arrived back in London after living in Southern California for several years. Having been surrounded by people who knew the power of prayer and especially the prayer of intercession, I was shocked by how hard it was to find praying people in London, a city as strategic and important as it is. It seemed in those days that even though Christianity was declared the national religion, Judeo/Christian values had grown silent, and the life of the church was either being lived out personally, mostly privately or publicly by following a format, increasingly growing outdated and irrelevant within the changing culture. Nothing was questioned or contended for, and no one dared to outstep being 'politically correct'. (I always thought I had been born and educated in a Christian nation, and, therefore, everyone was a Christian, and its capital would be built up by a group of bold, praying hearts.) Prayer was mostly hidden; even the largest churches in London had no regular prayer gatherings, where faith-filled Christian people declared goodness over the future. It was as if people lived in fear, unlearned in 'spiritual' correctness.

It was encouraging to me to soon see over 100 people gather to pray for this nation, first in Hampstead, and then a few years later with the Strategic Prayer School in Westminster, and see a ministry birthed called Prayer for the Nation, with yearly prayer summits that highlighted the importance of God's sons and daughters becoming informed intercessors, learning how to overcome any of their circumstances. Of course, that was a long time ago; nowadays it's easier to find bold prayer groups praying strategically, where you are able to join them, even worshipping and praying boldly and openly on our streets!

Prayer affects the future if you are feeling prompted to seek God's help each day. Whether you pray and worship from a standpoint of looking at life from the ground around you, or if you pray from a bird's eye view, this book will help you understand our spiritual history from the past, confidently live in the present, and boldly pray into the future.

Julie Anderson
The Prayer Foundation

ENDORSEMENTS

For some, the referendum on UK membership of the European Union has led our country into uncertain and uncharted waters. However, those of us who have a strong Christian faith recognise the power of prayer and the influence this can have in directing the UK towards a secure and prosperous future. God has an interest in the future of our nation and when we turn to Him in prayer, we really can make a difference - **2 Chronicles 7:14**

Sir Jeffrey Donaldson MP, Chairman Prayer for Parliament

Throughout history, the move of God's Holy Spirit through common men has been visible in events that have redirected the world…from Abraham and Moses to Martin Luther, William Wilberforce and Abraham Lincoln. In our lifetime, we have seen Hitler defeated in WW II and the Berlin Wall fall…both due, once again, to the Holy Spirit and His people through the power of intercessory prayer, as well as many who have given their lives to accomplish the Father's goal. Rees Howells was one of these vessels chosen by the Father to stand against Hitler. He spent countless hours in intercessory prayer gaining one place of faith after another, having been trained by the Holy Spirit his entire life for his high calling as an intercessor.

God's Hand in BREXIT is a thrilling account of a new move of the Holy Spirit. It follows our temporal and seen realm along with its spiritual and unseen counterpart. It begins with a group of Christians called to intercede and take a stand by faith for the heart and soul of England resulting in England exiting the European Union. BREXIT is only the beginning… for great intercession is also being made by the Britain Prayer Court for Israel, and England's relationship with her as her true heritage comes into being.

As an American watching our country go through the 2016 Presidential election, I was greatly encouraged by BREXIT and sensed that God would do the same thing here as He had done in England…leave the 'known land' and seek a new way.

BREXIT encompasses much more than prayer. "A body Thou hast prepared Me" (Heb. 10:5) speaks of Christ living and moving and having His being through our lives in order for God's love-purposes to be fulfilled on earth.

Rejoice in this book recounting the enormity of the work of the Holy Spirit in England, and watch in faith as the sons of God are revealed…bringing the body of Christ into its true identity.

DeeDee Winter
The USA

Deedee had a close friendship with Norman Grubb (Author of Rees Howells Intercessor) the last thirteen years of his life and hosts a website to his life and work...www.normangrubb. com. She has published seven books of his work...three of his personal correspondence and four of his writings and talks.

INTRODUCTION

In 2016, Great Britain experienced a historic referendum vote. The overall vote for Brexit represented the biggest shock to the political establishment in Britain and across Europe in decades.

It was reported that German Chancellor Angela Merkel called the vote "a watershed moment for Europe."

This book is about my adventures with Father God, and how I prayed and interceded with friends for our nation following the history-changing Brexit vote.

It is filled with rich and detailed reports of prophetic prayer times and prayer walks, when we cried out to the Lord to steer Great Britain along His intended path for this nation, a path which had been opened after David Cameron, the then Prime Minister, had decided that the British public should have the vote on whether to exit or remain in the European Union (EU).

The beginning of 2016 was a wake-up call for me, as the Lord opened my eyes to my identity and calling as His daughter, intercessor, and ambassador (see 1 Corinthians 7:20, 2 Corinthians 5:20, and Ephesians 1:18,19).

As I spent precious time seeking God's presence in prayer, He released into my heart the liberating truth of "Who I am" and "Who I am called to be," including a mother to my children, sister, aunt, friend, mentor, and professional sales executive. No, it was far beyond "me" and my own little world. Instead, it was growing into a deeper intimacy with God, discovering the power of prayer and intercession. How it can instantly change the tide of darkness that seeks to engulf Great Britain? As you read this book, I pray with all my heart that the Lord will awaken your calling and destiny as you grow into a deeper intimacy with Him.

The results of the Brexit vote caused seismic waves of reaction, shaking Great Britain to its core. Reactions included delight, relief, new hope, fear, hatred, confusion, division, anger, and economic rumblings, among others, but the Lord (the God of Abraham, Isaac, and Jacob) heard and continues to hear the prayers of the saints (Christians). He is faithfully working behind the scenes, as we fervently pray that our nation will turn in its God-given direction, outside of the EU, once again embracing its Judeo-Christian morals and heritage.

I have a dream that prayer and intercession for Great Britain become the norm for every Christian believer in this country, that we would become ablaze with light, signs, and wonders that dispel darkness in every sphere of society. Care homes would no longer be needed, as young people and the elderly renew an effective life balance such that families can take care of their loved ones. There would be less strain on the Great Britain National Health Service

(NHS), due to miraculous healing as believers lay hands on the sick; children in social care would be placed in loving families as believers adopt or foster them; young people's worth would be based on what the Lord sees in them, rather than the opinions of the media and celebrities. I pray that Great Britain becomes a nation that esteems God and upholds Him and His values, morality, opinions, and beliefs.

"For the creation waits in eager expectation for the children of God to be revealed"
Romans 8:19 (Amplified)

These are key times when the sons and daughters of the living God must rise and take their stand in unflinching prayer, intercession, action, and love. (see Isaiah 60:1).

My heartfelt prayer is for this read to be a catalyst to stir up the flame of God in you.

Thank you for reading.

Y.O. Cedar

WHY WE DID 40 DAYS OF PRAYER AT PARLIAMENT SQUARE

On a warm Saturday morning, the 25th of June, 2016, a couple of days after the nation had voted to Brexit from the EU, I was deeply troubled and distressed in my spirit because half the nation was in uproar, anger, and despair, rather than being united in gratitude and thankfulness for the outcome which was orchestrated by God. I was particularly disheartened that even within the body of Christ, we were divided.

Father God had appointed David Cameron as Prime Minister to give Great Britain the opportunity to decide whether to remain in or leave the EU. This was an opportunity for the body of Christ to seek the Lord's face and partner with Him through intercession and supplications to turn the tide and re-align Great Britain with its divine destiny.

And that's exactly what we did, along with a remnant of other believers across Great Britain. We sought the Lord's will and were amazed by His divine intervention. It was like in a dream, seeing Great Britain set free after being subjected to so many years of spiritual bondage under the EU. Great Britain had lost its identity as a Judeo-Christian nation. Multi-faith and secularism, rather than Christianity, had become the new norm, but the Lord, in His great love for us, had determined that His mercy would triumph over judgment.

What is The EU, Why Was It Created and When Was It Formed?

Why was the EU created?

After the Second World War, there was a new movement to create unity between Germany and France, which would ultimately lay the foundations for the European Union four decades later.

© Telegraph Media Group Limited 2016

When was the EU formed?

The EU can trace its origins from the European Coal and Steel Community (ECSC) and the European Economic Community (EEC), formed in 1951 and 1958 respectively by the Inner Six countries of Belgium, France, West Germany, Italy, Luxembourg and the Netherlands.

French foreign minister Robert Schuman led the formation of the ECSC with the Schuman Declaration in May 1950. The organisation was a forerunner of several other European Communities and what is now the European Union.

The European Union was established under its current name in 1993 following the Maastricht Treaty.

Since then the community has grown in size because of the accession of new member states.

The latest major amendment to the constitutional basis of the EU, the Treaty of Lisbon, came into force in 2009.

© Telegraph Media Group Limited 2016

This timeline outlines the previous results in referendums in European countries on joining the EC/EU from 1972 onwards

10 May 1972 **Ireland** **Turnout: 71%** YES 83% NO 17%	**3 October 1972** **Denmark** **Turnout: 90.1%** YES 63.3% NO 36.7%
26 September 1972 **Norway** Turnout: 79.2% YES 46.5% NO 53.5%	**20 November 1993** **Aaland Islands** Turnout: 49% YES 74% NO 26%
12 June 1994 **Austria** Turnout: 81% YES 66.4% NO 33.6%	**16 October 1994** **Finland** Turnout: 74% YES 57% NO 43%
27-28 November 1994 **Norway (again)** **Turnout: 88.7%** **YES 47,6%** **NO 52.4%**	**13 November 1994** **Sweden** **Turnout: 82.4%** **YES 52.2%** **NO 46.9%**
23 March 2003 **Slovenia** **Turnout: 60.3%** **YES 89.6%** **NO 10.4%**	**8 March 2003** **Malta** **Turnout: 91%** **YES 53.6%** **NO 46.4%**
10-11 May 2003 Lithuania Turnout: 63.4% YES 91.7% NO 8.9%	**12 April 2003** Hungary Turnout: 45.6% YES 83.8% NO 16.2%
7-8 June 2003 Poland Turnout: 58.9% YES 77.5% NO 22.6%	**16-17 May 2003** Slovakia Turnout: 52.1% YES 92.5% NO 6.2%

14 September 2003 **Estonia** **Turnout: 63%** **YES 66.9%** **NO 33.1%**	**15-16 June 2003** **Czech Republic** **Turnout: 55.2%** **YES 77.3%** **NO 22.7%**
20 September 2003 **Latvia** Turnout: 72.5% YES 67% NO 32.3%	**22 January 2012** **Croatia** Turnout: 43.5% YES 66.3% NO 33.1%
	23 June 2016 **United Kingdom** Turnout: 72.2% YES 48.1% NO 51.9%

Which countries are in the EU?

The European Union is an economic and political union of 28 countries. Each of the countries within the Union is independent but they agree to trade under the agreements made between the nations.

Twenty-two of the member states also belongs to the Schengen Area, which is comprised of 26 European countries that have abolished passport and border controls at their common borders. Of the countries that are not part of it, Bulgaria, Croatia, Cyprus and Romania all intend to join, while the United Kingdom and Ireland have opted out.

What is the purpose of the EU?

The European Union operates a single market which allows free movement of goods, capital, services and people between member states.

EU referendum | Sixty years of strained relations

From resistance to its entry and rows over contributions to monetary policy disputes and threats to leave, Britain has had a bumpy ride within the European Union.

1957 **Treaty of Rome is signed** France, West Germany, Italy, Belgium, Luxembourg and the Netherlands, six founding members of the European Economic Community, sign the Treaty of Rome, but Britain withdraws from early talks.	**1963** **France vetoes UK joining Common Market** With its economy flagging, Britain makes its first attempt to join the Common Market but is vetoed by Charles de Gaulle. The French President accuses Britain of a "deep-seated hostility" towards the European initiative.
1973 **Britain joins EEC** With de Gaulle out of office, Britain is allowed into the European Economic Community at last, but within a year calls for major reform of Common Agricultural Policy as well as changes in way the budget is financed.	**1983** **Michael Foot defeated** Labour leader Michael Foot promises withdrawal from EEC in his election manifesto, but his party is heavily beaten by Margaret Thatcher's Conservatives.
1975 **EEC referendum** Harold Wilson's Labour government holds a referendum over EEC membership, which splits the party but results on two-thirds of British voters saying they want to stay in.	**1984** **Thatcher wins Brussels rebate** A key victory for Mrs Thatcher sees her win a "rebate" from Brussels. She had threatened to halt contributions because Britain was receiving far less in agricultural subsidies than some other members, notably France.
1990 **Britain joins Exchange Rate Mechanism** Britain joins the Exchange Rate Mechanism, 11 years after it was set up to harmonise European countries' financial systems before the creation of a single currency.	**1997** **Single European Currency** Britain declares it will not be joining the euro for the duration of that parliament after the single currency fails Gordon Brown's 'five golden tests'.
1999 **British beef row** Tensions rise over France's ban on British beef during the "mad cow" disease outbreak. France given an ultimatum from Brussels but the ban is not lifted until years later.	**2007** **The Lisbon Treaty** Gordon Brown misses a televised ceremony of leaders signing Lisbon Treaty, which hands greater powers to Brussels. The controversial treaty took two years to negotiate after plans for an official constitution were abandoned.

2011 **Bank levy clash** David Cameron clashes with Europe over plans to introduce a levy on banks and restrict London's financial sector. The Prime Minister promises to bring back powers from Brussels.	**2013** **Cameron makes referendum pledge** David Cameron promises an "In-Out" referendum if he wins the 2015 general election, which he does. He reiterates his manifesto commitment to hold a referendum before the end of 2017.
February 2016 **EU referendum deal** David Cameron negotiates "new EU deal" for UK after 30 hours of talks but has to make series of concessions. The Prime Minister then announces the referendum will be held on June 23	**23 June 2016** **Referendum** In a close-run vote, the British public decides to exit the European Union. An emotional David Cameron resigns as prime minister the next day.

WHO WANTS TO STAY IN THE EU?

Prime Minister David Cameron is leading the campaign to remain in the 28-member group after securing a renegotiation over the terms of Britain's membership from his EU counterparts.

Among the terms of the agreement were restrictions on migrant benefits and an exemption from "ever closer" union.

Britain Stronger in Europe

The main group for the 'In' campaign is Britain Stronger in Europe - a cross-party group headed up by former Marks and Spencer boss Lord Rose. It had been awarded the 'official' campaign status from the Electoral Commission to lead the charge for those arguing the case for Britain to remain in the EU.

David Cameron had said Britain staying in the EU would make the country stronger, adding that the commonwealth countries felt Britain should stay after the other member states approved his terms for renegotiation.

The Prime Minister launched the official 'Conservatives In Europe for Britain' campaign along with fellow Cabinet members, although not all of his ministers were keen to be seen at the event.

Business secretary Sajid Javid and Home secretary Theresa May have said they will back the campaign to keep Britain in Europe but as both had their hesitations over the EU they were unwilling to be vocal in the campaign.

The Chancellor of the Exchequer has come out in favour of staying in the EU in light of Britain's renegotiated position, saying it would provide "the best of both worlds".

Osborne's main motivations are the benefits of free trade and the security of the EU without the costs of the eurozone. He claimed a vote to leave was a "huge leap in the dark".

In an exclusive op-ed for the Telegraph, the US president urged the UK to stay in the European Union.

Foreign Secretary Philip Hammond was seen as a possible candidate for defection but threw his support behind the Prime Minister after the renegotiations.

He said David Cameron's Brussels reform deal "tilts the balance" in favour of Britain staying in.

The Health Secretary Jeremy Hunt has come out in support of David Cameron's deal with Brussels, saying the country's sovereignty, economy, democracy, and human rights issues were stronger within the EU.

In a major blow for the Leave campaign, Sarah Wollaston has said that she now backs the case for staying in the EU.

The GP has claimed that Leave's central claims about a Brexit boosting the NHS are wrong and have convinced her to back the Remain campaign.

The Development Secretary Justine Greening has also signaled she is in favour of voting to stay in, calling the PM's renegotiation a "good deal".

The Immigration Minister is also backing the campaign to keep Britain in the EU, which given his department brief will have been strongly welcomed by the PM.

The Defence Secretary Michael Fallon says Britain needs a seat "at the table" of the EU and dismissed arguments that Britain will enjoy more sovereignty outside it.

The shadow Foreign Secretary will campaign for the 'In' campaign but said he will not share a platform with the PM.

Despite a few disagreements with Jeremy Corbyn, Benn and the Labour leader are united in wanting Britain to remain in the EU.

Corbyn said the Labour party would be campaigning for Britain to remain in the EU but criticised the PM's renegotiation, calling it a "missed opportunity to make the real changes we need" in Europe.

Labour's Alan Johnson is leading Labour's campaign to stay in the EU 'Labour In For Britain' while his leader Jeremy Corbyn has remained largely silent on the issue. If there is a debate on the issue, however, the former home secretary has said that like Hilary Benn he will not share a platform with David Cameron. The Labour campaign's security depends on its continued membership. The Labour campaign will be run separately to the cross-party Stronger in Europe campaign.

The London Mayor, Sadiq Khan and Labour politicians have argued it is in the interests of Londoners for Britain to remain in the EU.

Tim Farron, the Liberal Democrat leader is a strong advocate for Britain remaining in Europe - a position shared by his predecessor Nick Clegg.

Scotland's First Minister Nicola Sturgeon has said she believes most Scots will vote to remain in the EU - and that a Brexit would be a strong argument for a second Scottish Independence referendum.

The former Labour candidate and son of former Labour MP Jack Straw is the executive director of the cross-party Britain Stronger in Europe campaign.

WHO ARE THE GROUPS WANTING TO LEAVE THE EU?

Ahead of the EU referendum on June 23, campaigns have formed on both sides of the argument.

The Electoral Commission has designated Vote Leave as the "lead" campaign representing those wanting to leave the EU. The election watchdog said it based its decision base on a range of criteria such as the level of cross-party support, campaign tactics, and organisational capacity.

Vote Leave

Vote Leave is a cross-party campaign with support from all the main parties but based on Business for Britain, a pre-existing campaign group. Senior figures include Lord Lawson, the former Conservative chancellor. It is backed by senior politicians - including five Cabinet ministers - and is hoping to be named the official campaign for Britain to leave the European Union. Boris Johnson, Priti Patel, Douglas Carswell, Steve Baker, Bernard Jenkin are also among the senior politicians behind the campaign. It also has the backing of Labour Leave, which is headed by Labour donor John Mills.

Political strategists Matthew Elliott (who ran the campaign against the AV voting system) and Dominic Cummings, a former Conservative adviser, are occupying key backroom roles.

Grassroots Out

Vote Leave's main rival to be the official voice of the out campaign was Grassroots Out. The umbrella group sprang up early this year in response to the growing hostilities between Vote Leave and Leave.EU, another Out group largely supported by Ukip donor Arron Banks and Ukip supporters. It was started in January by Conservative MPs Peter Bone and Tom Pursglove and prominent Labour eurosceptic Kate Hoey MP.

The group has said it will hold local meetings in every constituency in the country for one hour each Saturday morning between now and the referendum in June.

It has the backing of long-standing Eurosceptic groups, some Conservative MPs and Ukip, as well as Nigel Farage and Respect Party leader George Galloway.

Who are the people campaigning to leave?

Nigel Farage, one of Britain's most prominent Eurosceptics, the Ukip leader has said we are better off outside the European Union.

Farage will no doubt play a prominent role in the campaign to leave the EU, despite his campaign group not being awarded official status.

The biggest political heavyweight to join the Out campaign is London Mayor Boris Johnson. Having previously claimed he is not an "outer", Johnson is perhaps the least likely Eurosceptic, and his family is also divided on the issue. His mother and brother are thought to be leaning towards the outside, while his sister and prominent pro-EU father have said they want to see Britain remain in the EU.

Johnson announced his decision to the media outside his house soon after letting the Prime Minister know by text but has denied claims it was part of a calculated move for the Tory leadership. In an interview with the Sunday Telegraph last week, he said that the European Union is pursuing a similar goal to Hitler in trying to create a powerful superstate.

Though a close ally of David Cameron and George Osborne, the Justice Secretary Michael Gove went against their wishes in putting his weight behind the Out campaign. He described the move as "the most difficult decision of my political life" but said his belief we are better off out of Europe stemmed from his time in Government and his belief that ministers are hamstrung by Brussels.

Liam Fox used a powerful speech at the Grassroots Out campaign's launch event to persuade voters to leave the European Union, saying he wanted to live in a country that was "an independent sovereign nation" again.

Owen Paterson, the Tory MP and former environment secretary has described the EU talks as "a sideshow" and insisted that Brexit is not "a leap into some terrible black abyss".

Iain Duncan Smith - one of the original Maastricht rebels - was one of the most committed and outspoken Eurosceptics in David Cameron's cabinet until he resigned in March. He has warned that Britain was "sailing perilously close to the rocks" by remaining in the European Union.

John Whittingdale, a known Eurosceptic, the Culture secretary is a council member of the think tank European Future, chaired by Grassroots Out member Tory MP Bill Cash and set up to oppose the Maastricht Treaty.

Despite once working as the European marketing director for a communications agency, Mr Chris Grayling is firmly in the Leave camp and was the first cabinet minister to speak out in an article in the Daily Telegraph. The Commons Leader said that remaining in the EU would be "disastrous" for Britain, and has gone on to warn ministers against scaremongering about Brexit.

A former MEP for six years before becoming an MP, Theresa Villiers bases much of her argument for wanting to leave the EU on her experiences in Brussels and before that as a lawyer. She has described leaving the EU as the "safer option".

Zac Goldsmith's father set up and funded the anti-EU Referendum party in 1995 and his Eurosceptic views influenced his son's take on the 28-state bloc and Britain's role within it. Goldsmith continued to campaign on Europe when he was running to be Mayor of London despite the capital's largely pro-EU stance.

The former press officer for the Referendum party, the anti-EU group funded by Zac Goldsmith's father, Ms Priti Patel has long-held Eurosceptic views based on a desire to regain control from Brussels.

A minister in Michael Gove's Justice department and an ex-aide to Grassroots Out supporter David Davis, Dominic Raab is a member of the EU Fresh Start group, set up with fellow Eurosceptic MPs. Raab has lambasted the Leave side for "scaremongering", quipping that it is "like Halloween came early".

George Eustice is one of the founding members of EU Fresh Start and stood as a Ukip candidate at the 1999 European Parliament elections.

Penny Mordaunt, the Armed Forces minister has gone against her boss Defence Secretary Michael Fallon in adding her voice to the Out campaign. "The oldest, most stable and most successful country in Europe has a duty to remind a European Union barely 50 years old that government is the servant, and not the master, of the people," she wrote in the Telegraph.

James Duddridge the Foreign Office minister has also gone against his superior, Foreign Secretary Philip Hammond, by joining the Brexit supporters.

Labour MPs Graham Stringer and Kelvin Hopkins were among those who set up Labour Leave, along with Labour donor John Mills, who still supports its umbrella campaign Vote Leave.

In the Bible, there are many instances of national crisis during which kings would ask the Lord for direction. As Great Britain sought answers based on their expert opinions and political agendas, I was saddened that none of them was asking for God's opinion on such a critical matter and that the Church didn't have a response, either. It was time for those who knew the Lord to humble themselves in prayer and fasting, seek the Lord in repentance and humility, and turn from their wicked ways so that the Lord would heal our land.

According to David Hathaway's research published in his book 'Babylon in Europe', (also in his documentary film, 'The Rape of Europe'), the European Parliament building in Strasbourg bears a strong resemblance to the shape of the Tower of Babel (as depicted in the oil paintings of Bruegel the Elder).

"Europe took its name from Europa, who, in Greek mythology, was raped by Zeus, who took the form of a bull. She became the "Queen of Heaven" and the EU regularly uses the image from Revelation 17 of this woman on the beast.

What is clear is that the EU deliberately set out to remove God from any of its foundational principles. The author shows how the decision to ban God from the Constitution was taken "behind closed doors, by an unelected group" (p. 47). All reference to God was removed, leaving only the values of godless humanism and exalted human reason to undergird the entire Constitution of Europe. As such, it is the spirit of Babylon that operates at the center of Europe".
DAVID HATHAWAY[1]

---

[1] Babylon in Europe and documentary film The Rape of Europe By David Hathaway

MY AWAKENING AS A WATCHMAN

As a Field Sales Executive, I'm accustomed to spending a lot of time in the car driving from one appointment to the next. My usual routine is to play worship music or listen to an audio Bible. For a while, I played the same CDs repeatedly, until one day when I'd had enough. However, rather than opt for another CD, I left the stereo on "Radio." And it happened to be tuned into Leading Britain's Conversation (LBC) Radio at the time David Cameron, the Prime Minister, was announcing that he was going to let Great Britain decide on its future regarding remaining in or leaving the EU. It was a decision later seen as Britain's biggest political decision in decades.

I sensed that a major turning point was about to take place, a crucial time for the body of Christ to seek God for His divine intervention and direction, as Great Britain's history was about to be reshaped. Prime Minister Cameron went on to say that the referendum vote would take place on June 23rd. Cabinet members and eligible members of the public would get to vote to determine Great Britain's future.

I continued to tune into LBC Radio to be aware of national issues and to stay informed regarding how to pray and prepare for the work of volunteer youth mentoring, which I was about to launch into.

A few weeks later, on April 5th, I was in the middle of listening to worship on my laptop when an email that Mrs.O, an intercessor from my local church, the Commonwealth Church Fellowship (CCF), came to my attention. The subject in the message said, "Temple of Baal will be erected in Times Square next month." More darkness to pray about! The moment I saw the headline, I gasped in shock and pondered how it was possible for something so openly demonic and occultist was to be accepted into today's society?

Below are some examples of what the Bible has to say about Baal:

> **"He did evil in the sight of the Lord and walked in the [idolatrous] way of his father [Ahab] and of his mother [Jezebel], and in the way of Jeroboam the son of Nebat, who made Israel sin. He served Baal and worshipped him, and he provoked the Lord God of Israel to anger, in accordance with everything that his father [Ahab] had done"** 1 Kings 22:52-53 (Amplified).

> **"Baal worship was rooted in sensuality and involved ritualistic prostitution in the temples. At times, appeasing Baal required human sacrifice, usually the firstborn of the one making the sacrifice"[2]**

---

[2] Got Questions Ministries on Bible Question Answer

"And have built the high places of Baal to burn their sons in the fire as burnt offerings to Baal, which I never commanded or spoke of, nor did it ever enter My mind (heart)" Jeremiah 19:5 (Amplified).

Intrigued, I clicked on the link in the email to find out more, only to discover, to my horror, that they intended to erect a replica at Trafalgar Square, as well. I knew instantly that this wasn't one of those times that you simply say a few prayers and expect change to happen. This required intense, mobilised, spiritual warfare. So, I thanked Mrs O for her email and suggested to her and the other intercessors included in the email that we needed to start a petition due to the significance of Trafalgar Square. Miss K responded by asking if I knew how to go about organising a petition, given my background in magazine publishing six years prior.

It was as if Miss K's simple question awakened something in the very core of my being. The next thing I knew, I was Googling for contact details and calling Andrea Minichiello Williams from Christian Concern for Our Nation (CCFON), to whom I hadn't spoken in many years. I knew that she would be able to point me in the right direction regarding mobilising a petition. I reasoned to myself that rather than start our own petition, we should avoid duplication and get behind CCFON, instead. Andrea said she wasn't circulating a petition, so she put me in contact with Lynda Rose at Voices for Justice (VFJUK), who was about to circulate a petition protesting the erection of the replica Baal Temple Arch at Trafalgar Square.

Lynda and I were immediately on the same spiritual wavelength during our phone conversation. I discovered that VFJUK was formed to defend the voiceless and speak the truth, to uphold justice. We agreed that I would get my church and many others behind her to sign the petition against the Mayor's office plans to erect the replica Arch at Trafalgar Square. A few hours later, a petition was drafted and sent to various believers using social media and mailing lists. At the same time, it occurred to me that we needed to mobilise strategic intercession, as this was a spiritual onslaught against our society. Petitioning was great, but without overcoming this through prayer, our efforts would be futile and short-lived, so I suggested this to Lynda, who agreed, but asked that I mobilise the prayer, rather than her, as she had a lot on her platter at the time. Prayer was something that I loved doing—and still is—so I agreed to spearhead and mobilise prayer with fasting that would lead up to a prayer walk at Trafalgar Square.

That same day, VFJUK published the following news press release: "Baal Replica Temple Erection at Trafalgar Square." They mobilised a petition to the Mayor of London, Boris Johnson, and Roger Michel, the Executive Director of the Institute for Digital Archaeology, not to celebrate the occult and to abandon the plans to reconstruct the Arch of Palmyra in Trafalgar Square on April 19th

In 2015, the pictures of destruction by ISIS/Daesh of the Temple of Bel (also known as Baal Shamin) in Palmyra rightly shocked the world, and attempts to safeguard the world's historical heritage from future acts of senseless aggression are to be applauded. However, the reconstruction of the temple arch in Trafalgar Square on April 19 by the Oxford-based Institute of Digital Archaeology (IDS) will serve a much darker purpose.

Roger Michel, the IDA's executive director, told The Times that, "It is really a political statement, a call to action, to draw attention to what is happening in Syria and Iraq … The symbolic value of these sites is enormous." At first glance, the sentiment appears unimpeachable. But a problem arises when considering the exact nature of the symbol being celebrated. From earliest times, Baal was a powerful symbol of evil and the occult, a pagan Canaanite god who demanded regular and bloody appeasement by child sacrifice. Baal worship, representing all that was evil, was particularly condemned in the Bible (e.g. Leviticus 18:21).

In terms of symbolic value, however, even more, disturbing is the date chosen for the reconstruction of the monument, because in occult belief, April 19 marks the Feast of Moloch, another ancient Canaanite god, specifically associated with Baal (e.g., Jeremiah 32:35), who also demanded child sacrifice. April 19 marks the first day of a thirteen-day period known as the "blood sacrifice to the beast," and culminates in the high occult holy day of Beltane on May 1st. It was a period regarded as hugely significant in the worship of Baal, dating back to Enmarkar, one of the ancient kings of Babylon—known in the Bible as Nimrod—who eventually came to be worshipped as a god.[3]

---

[3] Voices For Justice Press Release, 9 April 2016

Midnight Prayer Walk at Trafalgar Square

By God's design, nineteen intercessors responded to the call to pray by turning up at Trafalgar Square at midnight to repent on behalf of the body of Christ and the nation of Great Britain, to enthrone the King of Kings, and to declare His sovereignty over our nation.

As we prayed, the Lord revealed to us that due to the spiritual slumber of the body of Christ, the Baal (Bel) spirit and godlessness was already prevailing against our society, as the spirit was already in the hearts of many. This was evident through the increasing normalisation of sexual perversion and transgender concerns, with children as young as 4 years old being introduced into schools, lawlessness, child abuse and sex trafficking, child rebellion, and wickedness and depravity prevailing in all spheres of society, etc.

On the surface, it looked like we had no victory, as, sadly, only 10,000 believers signed the petition organised by Voices for Justice UK, so the replica Arch was, nonetheless, erected.

According to Roger Michel, the replica arch was built as part of a project by the IDA, a joint initiative that works with Oxford, Harvard, and the Museum of the Future in Dubai, the United Arab Emirates, to draw attention to the destruction of cultural artefacts across the world, and to rebuild some pieces.

THE AWAKENING OF INTERCESSORS

What the enemy planned for evil, God was turning around for His glory and for our good because the Lord used the incident to awaken us intercessors to take our place as watchmen over our nation.

Trafalgar Square is referred to as the heart of the nation of Great Britain. It is so central and significant to the country that the distances to other nations are measured from there. As we prayer walked, the Lord revealed the following spiritual truths to us, which you can use as a guide during your prayer time for your nation.

- Troubled Youth – The moment we arrived at the square to pray, we saw some young people fighting and the police had to come on the scene. This reflected the turmoil a lot of young people face today. We declared that the generation of the youth will walk in love and their true identities in Christ.

- Intimidation - We faced initial confrontation from the guards that we weren't allowed to sing. But we stood our ground and came to an agreement. We did our worship on the top of the stairs leading into the Square. This reflects the intimidation believers initially face when they choose to rise and confront the enemy.

- Repentance - Our repentance on behalf of the body of Christ led to a realigning of God's position as being enthroned over Great Britain's heart and, therefore, enthroned over the country.

- Armor of God - We declared Ephesians 6 and put on the full armor of God before standing in the gap to pray.

- Worship - We released worship in one accord in unity that ushered in the Lord's presence. As we did that, I saw in a vision that the square was surrounded by a wall of fire.

- We had a vision of the image of the dragon being contained.

- One of the intercessors marched around us with a flag that had symbols of fire on it.

- We had interference from three Muslims as they started shouting, "Allah! Allah! Allah!" We ignored them and continued to worship. They faded away, as the glory of the Lord fell upon us.

- A drunk young man stumbled/staggered and stood in our midst while we were praying.

- A homeless young man came up to say "Hello" to one of our intercessors.

- We took communion to reflect the oneness and unity amongst the body of Christ (the Lord's coming for a body, not a church denomination).

- We discerned that Trafalgar Square was also set out as a court before the Throne of Father God, where the enemy was judged and disarmed.

- Many of the natural memorials at the Square had a natural and spiritual significance.

- The four lions represented watchers who guarded the Nelson tower. In the same way, Father God has called us to watch and pray for the city and the nation. We declared that the lion of the tribe of Judah has dominion over the Square and our nation.

- Nelson's tower was set up to commemorate him dying in defense of the nation. There are also other monuments and plaques in the Square to commemorate other victories our nation won during battles. In the same way, Jesus died in our defense and to set us free. As the body of Christ, we commemorate this through the taking of communion. He lives forever to defend us and He calls us to defend the heritage He has given to us as a nation.

- Nelson's monument also signifies today's culture of exalting man rather than the Lord (e.g., the culture of celebrity worship).

- The seven pillars of society were greatly represented at Trafalgar Square, so we declared a redemption of them through the victory of Christ on the cross.

- Finance - Monument of horse skeleton with the footsie 100 – We broke the curse of financial turmoil and declared that Father God's war horse releases the spirits of financial integrity, wise stewardship, justice, and truth, which replace financial corruption, greed, exploitation, and robbery. We also prayed that the monument would be removed and replaced with someone or something representative of truth, justice, and righteousness.

- Art, Culture, and Entertainment – The national art gallery was built on the grounds and the Square is used greatly for entertainment.

- Government – Historically, election results were revealed here. Political rallies have also been held at Trafalgar Square, which is owned by Her Majesty, the Queen, and managed by the Greater London Authority (GLA).

- Media - Political demonstrations and national celebrations are reported here.

- Commerce – Trafalgar Square represents the crossroads of London.

- Religion - The square has been used to exalt the Lord (e.g., Passion of the Christ drama that takes place there once a year). There used to be a monument of a committed Christian, General Charles Gordon, His left hand holds the Bible and under his left arm is his cane. On each side of the pedestal is a bronze panel representing "Faith and Fortitude" and "Charity and Justice," respectively. For some reason, It was removed in 1943 and re-sited on the Victoria Embankment ten years later.

- Family - The Square is a family outing place.

- Education - History of Great Britain.

- The Square represents the soul of Great Britain. Whatever monument is erected there must be godly, lovely, praiseworthy, and pure.

- It has crossroads to every part of Great Britain. Pathway to other nations. We declared Trafalgar Square the "Highway of Heaven," with pathways of righteousness leading from it.

- Father God was giving increased discernment as we, the body of Christ, began to see with our spiritual eyes and hear with our spiritual ears and decree with our mouths that His purposes would establish His Kingdom in this land.

- We had a strong sense that there was currently a war raging over who would reign over our nation—Jesus Christ or the devil? And that the battle against the Baal Temple arch being placed in Trafalgar Square was representative of this conflict.

- Jesus yearns for Great Britain to return to Him. He is the One Who put the "Great" in Great Britain and poured out His blessings on the country, and yet it has increasingly turned its back on Him.

- I could feel such yearning and great sorrow over Britain's growing rejection of Jesus.

- Just off the Square, one can see some Union Jacks flying high from a rooftop.

- The flags are a clear reminder of Britain's very deep Christian roots. The British flag has not one, but two, crosses on it. The conventional cross, as we know it, plus the cross of Saint Andrew. The British flag is possibly the only flag in the world that has not just one. but two. crosses on it. What a statement of faith in Jesus!

- The devil wants to claim Trafalgar Square, the center of Britain (being literally at the center of London, the nation's capital), to display his "supremacy" and "great influence" over the country.

- At the front of Nelson's column in Trafalgar Square are Nelson's immortal words from the Battle of Trafalgar: "England expects that every man will do his duty." These words really leapt out at me and I felt God was speaking powerfully through them.

- We sensed Father God saying that Britain was facing another major war—a crucial war for Britain's soul—and that the Church must wake up and do its duty.

- Trafalgar Square commemorates the sacrifices of many others in the past for Britain's security and wellbeing. For example, Admiral Nelson sacrificed his life at the Battle of Trafalgar.

- Father God has saved Britain so often in the past, yet so many in our nation have turned their backs on Him.

- Just as we live in peace, freedom, and safety today because of the great sacrifices, great sense of duty, and courage of others in the past, so, too, today we, the Church, must be willing to make sacrifices and be courageous to win the war for Britain's soul, for the sake of God, and for the sake of this and future generations.

- We sensed that, whether we like it or not, we are at war and that it is growing in intensity. We did not start this war, but we as Christians must rise and defend our nation.

- Sadly, at present, much of Britain's Church is still fast asleep and some supposed Christians are even collaborating with the enemy!

- The Lord reminded us of the "military" verses in the Bible where the Apostle Paul exhorted Timothy to "fight the good fight" 1 Timothy 1:18 (Amplified) and be "like a good soldier of Christ Jesus" 2 Timothy 2:3 (Amplified), as well as "No soldier in active service gets entangled in the [ordinary business] affairs of civilian life; [he avoids them] so that he may please the one who enlisted him to serve" 2 Timothy 2:4 (Amplified.)

- As I noticed the fact that most of the statues in Trafalgar Square carry swords, I sensed God saying that we, too, as Christians must use our swords (i.e., Sword of the Spirit) in the present war for Britain's soul (see Ephesians 6:17).

- We should read Father God's Word regularly and extensively, and be very faithful to it and apply it obediently in our lives and the life of our nation.

- We should also declare Scripture in our prayers for our nation.

- I also had a strong sense that Father God is with us in this war. I sensed that He is far more present with us than we may even realize, and that everywhere we turn and look, He is there.

- The pools of water like streams of the Holy Spirit pouring out in the people of Britain— bring renewal, spiritual refreshing, spiritual life, and healing water over our nation.

- The many statues and plaques remind us that Father God has protected our nation in times past, and when, in the natural, things were against us.

- Prayer walks to be a normal part of life of every Christian, not only to gather in times of desperation, but also to establish an open Heaven. *"(an open heaven is when heaven touches earth. Jesus taught that this is the one true object of prayer when he instructed us to ask, "Your will be done on earth as it is in heaven". Which of us does not want this – to live under an open heaven, to revel in an unhindered experience of heaven on earth?)*[4]

- We must administer righteousness and justice in every part of London and every city in the UK.

- Ancient landmarks shall not be removed (see Proverbs 22:28).

- Prayer walking and prayer at key sites in London are needed on a regular basis.

- Prayer for Israel and Jewish people are linked with our prayers about the Palmyra arch, London, and Great Britain. We met up on Nisan 1, the start of the Jewish New Year. I was asked to blow the shofar at the end, so that the Lord could put His seal on our prayers and petitions, but I was unable to do so!

- At the end, Mr. B remarked, *"I asked the Lord for a miracle to blow the shofar and told myself not to worry because God could perform a miracle."* At that moment, at around 3am, three teenagers walked by our group as we prayed on the pedestrian area overlooking the center of the Square. One of them turned around and gently mocked, "I can blow better than that." "Go on then, you blow," and I offered the shofar to him. The teenagers turned and joined us. I gave him the shofar and God gave me discernment that they were Jewish. "Are you Jewish?" I asked. "Yes," one of them answered. I replied, "Shalom," and we shook their hands. We briefly shared our love for Israel and belief in the Messiah. They hadn't met friendly Christians like this before. Two of the teenagers' names were Daniel and Joseph. Sorry, but I didn't catch the name of the third teenager. "We've got to go. My mother will be getting upset," one of them said. I replied, "Go on. Please blow the shofar." Joseph held the shofar and

---

[4] Life Messenger (www.lifemessenger.org)

blew a loud, sustained sound. Praise God! We shook hands and they left. They were well behaved. They weren't drunk, just out for an evening together.

- What is the significance of all of this? We must pray for Israel and the Jews. Jews and Gentiles, the One New Man. Many Jews will receive the Lord in their hearts.

- The blowing of the shofar declared the extension of Father God's glory and domain.

LAUNCH OF BRITAIN PRAYER COURT

After the revelations and spiritual insight that we received at Trafalgar Square, we couldn't go back to slumber or complacency. It was clear to us that the Lord had used the erection of the replica Arch to stir us up to awaken to our calling as intercessors and spiritual watchmen to pray revival and reformation into reality. Thus, we continued to meet and pray once a week through Skype and, occasionally, go on prayer walks, as led by the Holy Spirit. So, in the lead up to the EU Referendum, we were already gaining momentum, keeping up to date with the news headlines, capturing Father God's heart, and interceding over our nation.

One day, Julie Anderson, my pastor and mentor, told me that we had to give the new prayer initiative a name, as it was a ministry that had its own entity. I prayerfully considered this. I come from a dysfunctional background and had been a single mother my entire adult life, so my heart's desire burned to see broken families restored, people to awaken to their true identities, morality upheld and used as a blueprint for society, not celebrities, media, or money. A nation filled with godliness, love, and peace, so with the Lord's help, the name "Britain Prayer Court" was birthed. Our mandate is to pray for revival and reformation to be established in Great Britain, a society where to do good for one another is the norm.

As I mentioned earlier, the nature of my job enables me to keep up to date with daily news, as I spend a lot of time driving to business appointments. So, we were quite knowledgeable on the issues and concerns of the people the whole time. It was interesting. One particular time, on February 16th, people began a debate on Leading Britain's Conversation (LBC) Radio following up on a news report that Prince William had appeared to signal support for remaining in the EU. It was reported that the Duke of Cambridge made a speech to British diplomats, emphasising the importance of partnership with other nations.

The Duke of Cambridge had said that Britain's ability to work with other nations is the "bedrock of our security and prosperity," in remarks that prompted speculation that he was endorsing the UK's continued membership of the EU.

Prince William told recipients of the inaugural Diplomatic Academy awards that, "In an increasingly turbulent world, our ability to unite in common action with other nations is essential. It is the bedrock of our security and prosperity and is central to your work."

Kensington Palace said the Duke was not talking about the EU. "This speech was not about Europe," a palace spokesman said. "He does not mention the word Europe once."

Great Britain paid close attention to what the Prince had said and comparisons made with remarks made by the Queen on the eve of the Scottish independence referendum in 2014 in which she asked voters to, "think very carefully about the future." I began to ask God for His thoughts on the EU Referendum. What was His will for Britain? Meanwhile, there was increasing tension concerning Great Britain's future. Immigration was at an all-time high, there was a crisis within the NHS, schools over-stretched, there was limited housing, unemployment, etc. Those of us with spiritual discernment began to recognise the window of opportunity for a move of God.

EU Prayer Summit – 18 June 2016

As Great Britain weighed things with their human reasoning and understanding, we began to perceive the spiritual implications. There was a bigger picture and purpose behind the EU Referendum vote.

As we inched ever closer to the date of the vote, I knew it was important to hold a prayer summit, during which we could all come together and pray in person. Although the last time I organised an event had been more than six years prior, I still knew how to put something together on a shoestring budget. I first sought the Lord's guidance and help to obtain the right venue.

For many years, I'd admired William Wilberforce for being a believer who was not afraid to stand for what he believed in and for using his platform in government for the advancement of God's Kingdom in eradicating the slave trade and for the society of manners and social reform. So, I earnestly sought the Lord's favour to host the summit at Moggerhanger Abbey, the place where William Wilberforce's cousin once lived and where the Clapham Sect had many strategic meetings, planning for the abolition of the slave trade. I also tried to secure a place to pray at The Clapham Church, the place of worship where William Wilberforce once attended, as I thought it would be nice to have the meeting at a venue with a rich history of hosting anointed meetings that birthed reformation in the past, but, again, to no avail. By now, time was running out and I didn't know what to do other than turning the matter over to the Lord. Then I heard Him say that the venue would be confirmed the following morning.

The next morning, I attended a strategic prayer meeting around Satanist ritualist abuse in the UK at the Emmanuel Centre. The moment I arrived, the Holy Spirit asked me to approach the event's manager to determine if we could hold the prayer summit there. I was immediately met with favour from John Tan, the manager, so on June 18th, in the heart of Westminster, the Lord mobilised intercessors of one heart and mind from across Great Britain to join us in intercession over the EU referendum vote. At this point, we knew the Lord's will for our nation was to leave the EU. In the beginning, I just had the impression on my heart that the Lord wanted us to be free, as the relationship with the EU was one of an ungodly alliance. We later became aware of different prophecies for Great Britain that confirmed what the Lord was saying to us. For example, **"Britain has a spiritual history and prophetic destiny," shared Mrs O at the prayer summit. She then went on to present to the prayer meeting the prophecies below:**

The true purpose of this referendum was not about jobs, immigration, trade agreements, or politics, but, rather, about God's plan and purpose for the UK.

Britain, as a small island off the coast of mainland Europe, brought the Gospel of Jesus Christ to practically the entire world. We knew the British Empire had many negative things about it, but its main purpose was God's purpose, that the Gospel of

Jesus Christ would be preached to the ends of the Earth, and that is exactly what happened.

Considering its size, Britain has a great history in the world.

One day recently, the Lord woke me up with a tune, which I later discovered was called "The Sailors' Hornpipe." It was a song that sailors sang on Navy ships.

From the mid -1700s until well into the 20th century, the British Royal Navy was the most powerful navy in the world, playing a key part in establishing the British Empire as the dominant world power from 1815 until the early 1940s. That was why Great Britain could dominate the world.

The Lord has also woken me up on other occasions with the songs "Rule Britannia" and "Edelweiss," which is a song about national sovereignty.

Why should it be that Britain, a relatively small nation, could be so powerful? Is it not because God was with her?

Britain was and is a Christian nation. It has taken the Gospel to the Commonwealth and to North America, which was founded by Christians from England.

And now, according to prophecy, Britain is key to the Gospel revival in Europe, and there have been many prophecies to that end.

No wonder the enemy wants to prevent that. The enemy wants Britain to be subdued and controlled by the anti-Christ spirit of Europe. That has always been the agenda behind the wars that Britain has fought in Europe.

During the Second World War, Hitler—who was anti-Christ—wanted to dominate all of Europe. In 1940, he planned the invasion of Britain, but God had intercessors—people including Rees Howells and his associates—praying.

And pray they did! And that invasion was miraculously averted.

Winston Churchill, in his War Memoirs, wrote of how, on September 15th, 1940, he visited the Operations Room of the Royal Air Force (RAF) and watched as the enemy squadrons poured over Great Britain, with the British planes flying up to meet them. A moment came when he asked the Air Marshal, "What other reserves have we?" The Air Marshal replied, "There are none." Then another five minutes passed, and, "it appeared that the enemy was going home. The shifting of the discs on the table showed a continuous eastward movement of German bombers and fighters. No new attack appeared. In another ten minutes, the action was ended." There seemed no reason why the Luftwaffe (German air force) should have turned for home, just at the moment when victory was in their grasp[5]

After the war, Air Chief Marshal Lord, Dowding, Commander-in-Chief of Fighter Command in the Battle of Britain, made this significant comment: "Even during the battle one realised from day to day how much external support was coming in. At the end of the battle, one had the sort of feeling that there had been some special Divine intervention to alter some sequence of events, which would otherwise have occurred".[6]

There have been many prophecies that have shown that Britain's role in bringing the Gospel to the nations is not finished with the Commonwealth, as it will move into Europe.

For example, in 1947, Smith Wigglesworth prophesied of distinct moves of the Holy Spirit in Britain in which the Word and Spirit would be brought together. A new move of the Spirit would take place in traditional churches, a new movement of churches would be birthed, and then a movement of the Word and Spirit into the continent of Europe would be birthed.[7]

Then, in 1967, the Lord showed a lady named Jean Darnell a move of God across the UK sweeping into Europe in which small churches were set ablaze. This was triggered by small groups of people praying across Great Britain, just as we are doing today.[8]

Forty years later, in 2007, at the Awaken Prophetic Conference held in London, hosted by Prayer For The Nation, Chuck Pierce prophesied that "'The enemy has a plan to suppress the vision of God in this land (i.e. England). There is an unholy alliance being negotiated now in this nation. I [God] have worked in times past to prevent this nation from forming this type of alliance. However, now it will be your choice whether you align wrongly or align with Me. I say to the people of England, you will be contending concerning this alliance. However, if they reject this alignment, they will find another alignment with Germany and France at their door.

He also went on to say, "Do not become complacent and sympathetic with the enemy that is in your land. If you do, your land will be overtaken. From the centre of this land, a gate is being formed. Determine at this gate whether he [Satan] will rule or I will rule. The rulership at the gate of England is being determined now!"

---

[5] Rees Howells-Intercessor' by Norman P Grubb Published by Lutterworth Press, London, 1973. Paperback edition. Chapter 35 page 261)
[6] Rees Howells-Intercessor' by Norman P Grubb Published by Lutterworth Press, London, 1973. Paperback edition. Chapter 35 page 261)
[7] As spoken by Malcolm Duncan at the Watching National Prayer Conference of the World Prayer Centre+
[8] As spoken by Malcolm Duncan at the Watching National Prayer Conference of the World Prayer Centre

So, from this, we can see that through participating in an alliance or union with France and Germany, the EU is an alliance with the enemy and against the purpose of God.

Malcolm Duncan is a minister who, during 2016, prophesied that 2017 marked 70 years since the Wigglesworth prophecy and 50 years since the Darnell prophecy. He had a sense that this was significant and that just as Daniel was awakened to the promise of God to Israel concerning an end to their 70-year captivity, so God was awakening him to God's desire to move in power in the UK church in 2017. In addition, 2017 marks 50 years after the Jean Darnell prophecy, the period of the jubilee in Israelite tradition.

Bearing these things in mind, Malcolm Duncan believed that there would be a fresh love of the Holy Spirit in the UK church in 2017 and one of the things that will happen, beginning in 2017 is that God will birth a passion for the Gospel that will spread from the UK across the continent of Europe. [9]

So, from all this we can see that Britain cannot fulfil God's purpose if it stays under the rulership of the EU, thus choosing to side with the enemy, rather than God.

Britain must "come out from among them" (2 Corinthians 6:17-18 (Amplified).

The church is not being asked to make a political choice on Thursday, June 23, 2016, when the nation votes on the EU Referendum, but a spiritual one. It is not a question of siding with the Conservatives, or Labour, or Liberal Democrats, or any other party. The question which British Christians must ask themselves is, do we want God's plan for this nation to be fulfilled or not? Whose side are we on?

I believe we are going to see a move of God in the UK in 2017 and that God is asking us to get ready. He is asking us to raise our faith and expectations, our commitment to prayer, and our eyes off what we are seeing around us, as well as to take our eyes off the feeling and the falling and the decaying, and to lift our eyes to Him. I also believe that this movement of God will contain six significant elements, including the following:

1. He will expose the hearts of those in our churches who currently have been churched, but not saved.

2. He will strengthen the hearts of those who love Christ, including men such as Justin Welby and Pope Francis.

3. I believe that God is going to revive and strengthen small local churches, that He is going to give new confidence, hope, purpose, and meaning to what you and I would

---

[9] A prophetic word shared for the Church by Malcolm Duncan, National Prayer Conference, March 2016. (http://www. worldprayer.org.uk/world-prayer-centre-news/item/8120-prophetic-word-for-the-church-malcolm-duncan

describe as an ordinary church. That it is not going to be the big central churches with thousands of congregants which will herald what God wants to do, but, rather, it will be a birthing of new hope, energy, expectation, and passion in small local congregations. I don't believe that it will end in 2017, but, rather, it will start in 2017.

4. I believe that God is going to give us a fresh confidence in the Gospel, that He will give us a fresh openness to the Holy Spirit, as we delve into His Word.

5. God is going to give the broader Church a deeper yearning for prayer for the nation and the lost.

6. Lastly, God is to birth a passion for the Gospel to spread from the United Kingdom across the continent of Europe.

ACTIVITY: SOME PROPHETIC DECLARATIONS USED AT THE PRAYER SUMMIT

Following up on what Mrs O shared regarding UK prophecies previously, the Lord led us to repent at each of the seven gates of society (i.e., the pillars that underpin society: family, faith, government, education, arts and entertainment, media, and economy) and for not rightly aligning with Israel. We then enthroned the Lord over Great Britain with heartfelt praise and worship and declaring His Word of redemption over each area of society. You can use the same declarations and decrees as a guide during your own time of intercession over Great Britain.

FAMILY

HUSBANDS:

<u>Repentance for</u>: Failure of men to love their wives as Christ loves the church; lack of unconditional love; not yielding to the Lord; lack of protection or provision; failure to lead or support; abuse; disrespect, honour; divorce; neglect; abandonment; unfaithfulness; jealousy; discord, strife, lack of forgiveness; bitterness; dishonesty; greed; slumber; laziness; self-centeredness; double-mindedness (wavering in mind); and people pleasing, rather than God-pleasing.

<u>Declarations</u>: Husbands should: Love their wives, as Christ loved the church and gave Himself up for her; live surrendered, yielded lives to Christ; live with their wives in an understanding way, showing honour to the woman; love their wives and do not be harsh with them; love their wives as their own bodies; willingly provide for their wives; protect their wives; work hard, fear God, and honour their wives; be faithful, honest, gentle, and caring toward their wives; and pray and have devotions together with their wives.

WIVES:

<u>Repentance for</u>: Not putting God first; lack of unconditional love; not yielding to the Lord; dishonor; disrespect; abuse; divorce; neglect; abandonment; unfaithfulness; jealousy; discord / strife/ lack of forgiveness; bitterness; dishonesty; greed; slumber; laziness; self-centeredness; double-mindedness (wavering in mind); people pleaser, rather than God pleaser; and withholding love making / love.

<u>Declarations</u>: Wives should: Submit to husbands, as to the Lord; she does him good, and not harm; provide husband with unconditional love; look after the affairs of the home and do not be idle; be trustworthy and honor her husband; be respectful, faithful, honest, gentle, and caring for her husband; pray and have devotions together with her husband; be nurturing, supportive, and kind to her husband; pray for her husband; work hard; treat her husband like a king; make effort to look good for husband; be quick to forgive and do not dwell on wrongs and do not use children as pawns during times of family breakdown.

PARENTS:

<u>Repentance for:</u> Having babies out of wedlock; abortion; failure to train children in the way of the Lord; not modelling Christ to their children; neglect; abuse (emotional, physical, mental,

and sexual); abandonment; rejection; negative words; lack of support, encouragement, and affirmation; failure to protect, lead, and guide; harshness; impatience; exasperating children; failure to discipline; spoiling children; setting poor examples for children; exposing children to wickedness; not being transparent; double standards; strife, discord, and disharmony in the home; and putting ministry or work before children.

Declarations: Parents should: Love unconditionally; use the appropriate love language; honor and respect their children; train up their children in the way they should go, and even when they are old, they will not depart from it; not provoke their children to anger, but bring them up in the discipline and instruction of the Lord; tell their children about Father God and his ways and let their children tell their children, and their children's next generation, etc.; not conceal themselves from their children; tell their children to praise the Lord, His strength, and His wondrous works that He has done; manage their household well, keeping their children under control with all dignity; provide, protect, pray, support, and nurture their children; model Christ; be approachable, gentle, and discipline their children in love; be loving and nurturing at home; get involved in their children's lives (social, education, friends, peers, etc.); affirm their children; give their children a sense of belonging, acceptance, and value.

We also declare an increase in family discipleship programs and innovative ways of ministering to families. For instance, babysitters (e.g., Winston Churchill's nanny, Elizabeth Ann Everest, was an intercessor who prayed daily and instilled moral guidance), day care centers / nurseries, etc. who/that manifest the Kingdom of God; encourage foster families / adoptions to become place of refuge for the wounded and rejected; secure free legal help for divorcees; be asked to attend free marital counselling; first be Christian practitioners working more closely with Christian judges in position to advocate for families; conduct Kingdom family discipleship course, counselling, and advocacy; restore true identities and knowledge of Father God; develop strategies to minister to the LGBT (lesbian/gay/bisexual/ transgender) community, as well as dysfunctional and broken families; and demonstrate grace and strategies to model Christ to families around us, in schools, etc.

Arts and Entertainment

We repent:

- For failing to govern, release Kingdom, and effectively influence the arts and entertainment culture that brings social transformation.

- For creating a secular and sacred divide.

- For failing to engage in arts and entertainment for fear of contamination.

- For failing to recognise and exercise our power and influence as dispensers of God's love and grace in this industry.

- For failing to evangelise and share God's love with the lost in the arts and entertainment industry.

- For failing to effectively witness in the arts and entertainment arena through our own God-given gifts.

- For discouraging others from using their creative gifts to glorify God and share the Gospel through arts and entertainment

- For failing to effectively model godliness, purity, and morality through the arts and entertainment industry.

- For failing to produce wholesome, creative, and cutting-edge content through TV, film, theatre, music, fashion, comedy, journalism, art, and gaming.

- For failing to sufficiently fund Kingdom projects in arts and entertainment.

- For failing to fully release a Kingdom influence and the mind of Christ through arts and entertainment.

- For failing to exercise authority in this mountain.

Therefore, we also repent for allowing the demonic realm to advance its purposes and plans in the arts and entertainment industry on our watch. Please forgive us for:

- The increasingly demonic content and programming found in arts and entertainment, including TV, film, theatre, music, fashion, comedy, magazines, gaming, and other forms of entertainment.

- The alarming rise of pornography in arts and entertainment.

- The lack of available wholesome, life-affirming content.

- The advancement of blasphemy in arts and entertainment.

- The advancement of violent content in entertainment.

- The advancement of other religions, secularism, and humanism in arts and entertainment.

- The desensitisation of people toward sexual immorality, perversion, and violence in arts and entertainment.

- The advancement of the LGBT agenda in arts and entertainment.

- Helping to knowingly / unknowingly fund a demonic agenda in arts and entertainment through our finances through licensing and taxes.

We break every stronghold of the enemy over arts and entertainment and:

- Pray against ALL ungodly art and entertainment, and bind up every power and principality operating over this mountain.

- Bind up the work of the enemy in the unseen realm over this mountain and command complete confusion in the enemy's camp.

- Dismantle the work of the Jezebel spirit at work in arts and entertainment.

- Unloose every restraint upon Kingdom-oriented arts and entertainment.

- Unloose unprecedented favour, Kingdom resources, and abundant finance over the mountain of arts and entertainment for the advancement of the Gospel.

- Unloose cutting-edge Kingdom creativity and excellence in arts and entertainment to transform lives and reveal the love of God.

We thank You for:

- Expressions of God still maintained in arts and entertainment such as nativity plays, the resurrection story, and biblical-themed Hollywood films.

- Christians in arts and entertainment, including musicians, dancers, designers, journalists, actors, producers, artists, models, and writers.

- The cutting-edge, God-breathed projects currently being released in the arts and entertainment industry.

- The supernatural release of Kingdom resources, boldness, wisdom, and excellence.

- The ministries activity taking ground in this mountain.

- A turning in the tide and a reclamation of the arts and entertainment mountain as consecrated to God, for His glory and His redemption plans.

We declare and decree:

- That the rulers and authorities—those supernatural forces of evil operating against You—in arts and entertainment have been triumphed over, through the cross (see Colossians 2:15).

- That we will once again take up our posts as intercessors and spiritual gatekeepers within the arts and entertainment mountain (see Ezekiel 22:30).

- That we will allow only that which is true, whatever is noble, whatever is right, whatever is pure, whatever is lovely, whatever is admirable—if anything is excellent or praiseworthy; only such things will be glorified in arts and entertainment. (see Philippians 4:8).

- That You, God, have purposefully raised up artisans, creatives, and entertainers who are filled with the Spirit of God, who are skilled and knowledgeable to glorify You with excellence, beauty, and flair in arts and entertainment (see Exodus 35:30 - 36:1).

- That we boldly govern this mountain, for we are Your workmanship [Your own master work, a work of art], created in Christ Jesus [reborn from above—spiritually transformed, renewed, ready to be used] for good works in arts and entertainment, which God prepared [for us] beforehand [taking paths which He set], so that we would walk in them [living the good life which He prearranged and made ready for us] (see Ephesians 2:10).

- We will boldly proclaim Your light in the darkest parts of this mountain (see Isaiah 60:1) and proclaim Your excellencies, wonderful deeds, virtues, and perfections, for You, God, have called us out of darkness into Your marvellous light (see 2 Peter 1:9).

- That we will be ministers of reconciliation upon this mountain (see 2 Corinthians 5:18).

- That we do not lack any good thing as we govern this mountain (see Ephesians 1:3 and Psalms 34:10).

- That You will supply all the resources needed to produce anointed, cutting-edge creative arts and entertainment (see Philippians 4:19 and Ephesians 3:20).

GREAT BRITAIN AND ISRAEL

The Lord's declaration over Israel

"And I will make of you a great nation, and I will bless you [with abundant increase of favours] and make your name famous and distinguished, and you will be a blessing [dispensing good to others]. And I will bless those who bless you [who confer prosperity or happiness upon you] and curse him who curses or uses insolent language toward you; in you will all the families and kindred of the earth be blessed [and by you they will bless themselves] Genesis 12:2 (Amplified)

"The Scripture, foreseeing that God would justify the Gentiles by faith, proclaimed the good news [of the Savior] to Abraham in advance [with this promise], saying, "In you shall all the nations be blessed." Galatians 3:8 (Amplified).

God's Covenant with Israel

"I will establish My covenant (everlasting promise) between Me and you, and I will multiply you exceedingly [through your descendants]." Then Abram fell on his face [in worship], and God spoke with him, saying, "As for Me, behold, My covenant is with you, And [as a result] you shall be the father of many nations. "No longer shall your name be Abram (exalted father), But your name shall be Abraham (father of a multitude); For I will make you the father of many nations.

6 I will make you exceedingly fruitful, and I will make nations of you, and kings will come from you. I will establish My covenant between Me and you and your descendants after you throughout their generations for an everlasting covenant, to be God to you and to your descendants after you. I will give to you and to your descendants after you the land in which you are a stranger [moving from place to place], all the land of Canaan, as an everlasting possession [of property]; and I will be their God." Genesis 17:2-8 (Amplified).

"T then the Lord will drive out all these nations from before you, and you shall dispossess nations greater and mightier than you. Every place on which the sole of your foot treads shall become yours; your territory shall be from the wilderness to Lebanon, and from the river, the river Euphrates, as far as the western sea (the Mediterranean)" Deuteronomy 11:23-24 (Amplified).

The Balfour Declaration

The Balfour Declaration was a letter dated November 2, 1917, from the UK's Foreign Secretary, Arthur James Balfour, to Walter Rothschild, 2nd Baron Rothschild, a leader of the British Jewish community, for transmission to the Zionist Federation of Great Britain and Ireland. It read:

> His Majesty's government view with favour the establishment in Palestine of a national home for the Jewish people, and will use their best endeavours to facilitate the achievement of this object, it being clearly understood that nothing shall be done which may prejudice the civil and religious rights of existing non-Jewish communities in Palestine, or the rights and political status enjoyed by Jews in any other country. (The text of the letter was published in the press one week later, on 9 November 1917). The "Balfour Declaration" was later incorporated into both the Sèvres peace treaty with the Ottoman Empire, and the Mandate for Palestine.[10]

Replacement Theology

A typical definition of "Replacement Theology" can be paraphrased as, "Israel has been replaced by the Christian Church, so the promises and prominent position once held by God's chosen people are now held exclusively by the Church, said Elder D at the Prayer Summit."

"But if some of the branches were broken off, and you [Gentiles], being like a wild olive shoot, were grafted in among them to share with them the rich root of the olive tree, 18 do not boast over the [broken] branches and exalt yourself at their expense. If you do boast and feel superior, remember that it is not you who supports the root, but the root that supports you. You will say then, "Branches were broken off so that I might be grafted in." That is true. They were broken off because of their unbelief, but you stand by your faith [as believers understanding the truth of Christ's deity]. Do not be conceited, but [rather stand in great awe of God and] fear [Him]; for if God did not spare the natural branches [because of unbelief], He will not spare you either. Then appreciate the gracious kindness and the severity of God: to those who fell [into spiritual ruin], severity, but to you, God's gracious kindness—if you continue in His kindness [by faith and obedience to Him]; otherwise you too will be cut off. And even they [the unbelieving Jews], if they do not continue in their unbelief, will be grafted in; for God has the power to graft them in again. For if you were cut off from what is by nature a wild olive tree, and against nature were grafted into a cultivated olive tree, how much easier will it be to graft these who are the natural branches back into [the original parent stock of] their own olive tree? I

---

[10] The original document is kept at the British Library

do not want you, believers, to be unaware of this mystery [God's previously hidden plan]—so that you will not be wise in your own opinion—that a partial hardening has [temporarily] happened to Israel [to last] until the full number of the Gentiles has come in; and so [at that time] all Israel [that is, all Jews who have a personal faith in Jesus as Messiah] will be saved; just as it is written [in Scripture], The Deliverer (Messiah) will come from Zion, He will remove ungodliness from Jacob." "This is My covenant with them, When I take away their sins" Romans 11:17-27 (Amplified)

THE PRIME MINISTER: DAVID CAMERON

In February, at a debate in the House of Commons, it was reported that the Prime Minister had been asked by Labour MP Imran Hussain what the Government was doing "to prevent the infringement into Palestinian lives"

And Prime Minister Cameron replied, "I am well known for being a strong friend of Israel, but I have to say the first time I visited Jerusalem and had a proper tour around that wonderful city and saw what had happened with the effective encirclement of East Jerusalem, occupied East Jerusalem, it is genuinely shocking." He told the MP's.[11]

> **"I am not ashamed of the gospel, for it is the power of God for salvation [from His wrath and punishment] to everyone who believes [in Christ as Savior], to the Jew first and also to the Greek"** Romans 1:16 (Amplified)

> **"Behold, I am going to take the children of Israel from among the nations where they have gone, and I will [c]gather them from every side and bring them into their own land; 22 and I will make them one nation in the land, on the mountains of Israel; and one [d]king will be king over all of them; and they will no longer be two nations, and will no longer be divided into two kingdoms"** Ezekiel 37:21-22 (Amplified).

> **"Listen carefully, I will lift up My hand to the [Gentile] nations And set up My banner to the peoples; And they will bring your sons in the fold of their garments, And your daughters will be carried on their shoulders"** Isaiah 49:22(Amplified).

God's Command to Us

> **"Pray for the peace of Jerusalem: "May they prosper who love you [holy city]. "May peace be within your walls. And prosperity within your palaces." For the sake of my brothers and my friends, I will now say, "May peace be within you." For the sake of the house of the Lord our God [which is Jerusalem], I will seek your (the city's) good"** Psalms 122:6-9 (Amplified).

One New Man

> **"Therefore, remember that at one time you Gentiles by birth, who are called "Uncircumcision" by those who called themselves "Circumcision," [itself a mere**

---

[11] Information available at www.parliament.uk

mark] which is made in the flesh by human hands— remember that at that time you were separated from Christ [excluded from any relationship with Him], alienated from the commonwealth of Israel, and strangers to the covenants of promise [with no share in the sacred Messianic promise and without knowledge of God's agreements], having no hope [in His promise] and [living] in the world without God. But now [at this very moment] in Christ Jesus you who once were [so very] far away [from God] have been brought near [a]by the blood of Christ. For He Himself is our peace and our bond of unity. He who made both groups—[Jews and Gentiles]—into one body and broke down the barrier, the dividing wall [of spiritual antagonism between us], by abolishing in His [own crucified] flesh the hostility caused by the Law with its commandments contained in ordinances [which He satisfied]; so that in Himself He might make the two into one new man, thereby establishing peace. And [that He] might reconcile them both [Jew and Gentile, united] in one body to God through the cross, thereby putting to death the hostility. And He came and preached the good news of peace to you [Gentiles] who were far away, and peace to those [Jews] who were near. For it is through Him that we both have a [direct] way of approach in one Spirit to the Father." Ephesians 2:11-18(Amplified).

Removal of the Veil

"But [in fact] their minds were hardened [for they had lost the ability to understand]; for until this very day at the reading of the old covenant the same veil remains unlifted, because it is removed [only] in Christ. But to this day whenever Moses is read, a veil [of blindness] lies over their heart; 16 but whenever a person turns [in repentance and faith] to the Lord, the veil is taken away." 2 Corinthians 3:14-16 (Amplified)

Repentance

- God gave Great Britain a mandate to see the establishment of Israel based on the Word of God, but we handed this mandate over to the United Nations.

- Passivity, indifference, and inaction with regard to Hitler's decision to annihilate the Jews of Europe.

- The body of Christ in Great Britain has not fully recognised God's everlasting covenant with Israel.

- The body of Christ in Great Britain has propagated Replacement Theology.

- David Cameron's uninformed comments under pressure regarding the effective encirclement of East Jerusalem.

Declarations

As the body of Christ in Great Britain, we represent this great nation and declare:

- That Great Britain blesses Israel and recognises Israel as the covenant nation of God and that Great Britain, as a nation, chooses to align with Israel and break any covenant with nations bound to any other gods, for we declare, The Lord, He is God!

- That Great Britain and the body of Christ in this country shall help and support all Jews who obey the Word of the Lord to return to the land given to them by the Lord in obedience to the Word of God.

- That Great Britain will provide the life-giving truth of the Word and appropriate tools to introduce the Jews to their Messiah, Yeshua!

- That we will pray for the peace of Jerusalem as the Word of the Lord commands us to.

Pray:

- That the Jews will turn their hearts fully to the Lord in repentance, seeking His face and trusting in Him.

- For the blindfold to fall off the eyes of the Jews and that they would recognise and receive Yeshua as their sovereign Lord and Messiah.

Media

The Hittites descendants of Noah represent the spirit of fear. The strongman to be dethroned/decapitated is Abbadon/Pollydon "The Destroyer," known as the angel of the abyss (see Revelation 9).

The assignment of this king of the media mountain is to break down nations (people) with actual physical violence and/or violation of their minds with confusion and fear, with the intention to make afraid, discourage, cause dismay, to scare and terrorize, thus resulting in the people's phobias, heart attacks, nightmares, doubt, mistrust, and fear of death.

The enemy is using the media to cause fear to ultimately gain control of people today. As technology intelligence increases throughout television, radio, film, books, newspapers, and the Internet and social media, we must be alert to the enemy using these technologies to compete for possession and control of people's hearts, minds, and souls.

Idolisation

Admiration of celebrities and the materialistic. Amounting to people worship, as well as possessions, including cars, houses, jewellery, etc. This provokes feelings of dissatisfaction and inadequacy. Media are used to entice us to spend money on unnecessary items, thus trapping us in the bondage of debt by the seduction of must-haves that superficially and only temporarily provide gratification, but disguise the long-term pain and suffering of the consequences of believing the enemy's lies and deception.

Forgiveness: Lord Jesus, we ask for forgiveness for having idolised people by looking to them for answers, favour, and approval. Lord Jesus, forgive us for desiring possessions for the wrong motives to satisfy our egos in the belief that they make us appear successful and attract admirers to ourselves.

Declarations: In Jesus' name, we bind the lies and deceptions over our identities and loosen faith and belief of who we are in Christ Jesus, created to walk and live habitually in the Holy Spirit. We declare that we are not controlled by spirits and principalities of the darkness, but, rather, guided by the Spirit of our Living God. Therefore, we are not tempted to gratify cravings and desires of the flesh.

Commercialisation

Greed and exploitation of the weak, vulnerable, the poor in spirit. Fear of lack. Advertising using sexuality and fearful persuasion into purchasing products. Some of these companies are founded in harmful substances like tobacco, pornography, and slave labour.

Forgiveness: We ask for forgiveness for lusting with our eyes for worldly possessions that tempt us from Your promises over our lives, for our weaknesses and self-deception in persuading ourselves that we have been justified.

Declarations: In Jesus' name, we bind the spirits of greed, consumerism, and unrighteous ill-gotten gain. We bind the spirits of jealousy, envy, and addictiveness.

> **"Lord will open for you His good treasure house, the heavens, to give rain to your land in its season and to bless all the work of your hand;"** (Deuteronomy 28:12 (Amplified).

> **"Delight yourself in the Lord, And He will give you the desires and petitions of your heart"** Psalms 37:4 (Amplified).

Glamorisation of Immorality and Promiscuity

We are putting our children and youth at risk, emotionally and physically, through the misappropriation of healthy relationships using such sensualized messages, contrived to arouse and encourage perverse behaviour. Previously, books like "Fifty Shades of Grey" would have been censored, had their covers concealed, and been placed on the top shelf, where children and youth could not reach them. Yet, today, the media boldly published this book and even implied that if someone had not read it, then that person was missing out on something fantastic or there was something wrong with that person. Never mind the publicity over the queues outside cinemas when the main attraction film comes out. And now people can see such books and DVDs within a child's reach, at his/her height level in supermarkets and gas stations. Worse yet, one can download this and other inappropriate viewing and reading material on Amazon.com and opt to watch trailers and "look inside" books, thus taking a person's choice from such material's contents. There doesn't appear to be a filter in place for children and youth under the age of 18.

Forgiveness: We ask for forgiveness for not being godly role models to our children, the next generations, and our peers; for thinking we are above the law and putting our children and youth at risk; that in our own liberty, we have created stumbling blocks and in so doing, we opened doors inviting the weak and vulnerable to sin; for not doing more in prayer and actions for protecting them from these vile attacks of the enemy. God, forgive us for being hypocritical and not walking with integrity and righteousness, expecting our children to do what they are told and not what they see us and others doing.

Declarations: In Jesus' name, we bind the spirits of Jezebel, pornography, and desires for Babylonian thrills and entertainment. We loosen a hunger for healthy and fun and leisure activities, for discernment to perceive what is of You, God, and what is disguised harm from the enemy. We declare and decree that from Your Word:

> **"Older men are to be temperate, dignified, sensible, sound in faith, in love, in steadfastness [Christ like in character]. Older women similarly are to be reverent in their behavior, not malicious gossips nor addicted to much wine, teaching what is right and good, so that they may encourage the young women to tenderly love their husbands and their children, 5 to be sensible, pure, makers of a home [where God is honored], good-natured, being subject to their own husbands, so that the word of God will not be dishonored. In a similar way urge the young men to be sensible and self-controlled and to behave wisely [taking life seriously]"** Titus 2:2-6 (Amplified)

Proverbs 22:6 Train up a child in the way he should go [teaching him to seek God's wisdom and will for his abilities and talents], Even when he is old he will not depart from it (Amplified).

Mobilisation of Violence and Perversion

Some sensitive censorship prevails with national television, accompanied by warnings that "some viewers may find this material distressing," etc. However, with the ever-increasing technology of applications (APPS), unregulated Internet accessibility, and uploading, events can now be streamed live from a telephone straight to social media sites such as Facebook. In the wrong hands, this technology could be used for bullying, violent attacks, sexual abuse of a child, and explicit child and adult pornography, etc., thus causing further demoralisation and severe trauma or, even worse, death. About 53% of 11- to 16-year-olds have seen explicit material online, nearly all of whom (94%) had seen it by 14, the recent Middlesex University study says. The research, commissioned by the NSPCC and the children's commissioner for England, said many teenagers were at risk of becoming desensitised to pornography.

On May 5th, 1964, Mary Whitehouse declared in a meeting rallying support to bring about a radical change in the policy of entertainers, in general, and the Governors of the British Broadcast Commission (BBC), in particular, that, "In view of the terrifying increase in promiscuity and its attendant horrors, we are desperately anxious to banish from our homes and theaters those who seek to demoralize and corrupt our young people." Whitehouse prophetically warned the nation that, "If violence is shown as normal on the television screen, it will help to create a violent society."[12]

Many people who had a respected social standing and governmental influence, criticised and mocked Whitehouse. The likes of Roy Hattersley and others have since publicly admitted that they were wrong. Dame Joan Bakewell also did a U-turn, suggesting that the results of sexual liberation in the 1960s may not have had a positive effect for later generations.[13]

Forgiveness: Lord God, forgive us for not listening to the prophets and wise counsel. Forgive us for taking the broad path, so broad, in fact, that we were able to persuade many to join us, leading them also into temptation, instead of righteousness and godly living. Forgive us for our part in the demise of broadcasting by not being sober, or vigilant; for not heeding Your warning that our adversary, the devil, is as a roaring lion, walking about, seeking whom he may devour.

Declarations: We declare and decree that we have the mind of Christ. With integrity and uprightness, we walk in fear of the Lord away from the crooked, treacherous path of violence and perversion (see Proverbs 11:3).

We thank You, God, that Your love for us prevails, that You have never left us or forsaken us. Amidst the works of the devil, You have ensured that we do not lack and have made readily available Christian-based novels, films, and TV (God TV, Revelation, Hillsong, etc.). We thank You for the miracles of invention so You can reach the world with the Bible—already translated into 531 languages—through the Internet and satellite.

Abomination

Media flaunting in the face of God the very things that He writes are an abomination. Ordained ministers openly engaging in same-sex relations in family television programs. They are preachers and wearing a dog collar, so even though the programmes are fictitious, they are representative more and more of real life, thus rendering such programming and activities more acceptable, with people, in general, becoming more passive and complacent about such programming and activities.

Forgiveness: Lord God, forgive us for our complacency and fear of people for turning a blind eye to the blatant tactics of the enemy. Forgive us that our eyes and ears have turned dim and our hearts have hardened toward You. Forgive us for not seeking Your wisdom and trusting You to give us the words to speak in due season.

---

[12] See Mediawatch Uk for more information. http://www.mediawatchuk.com/our-history/
[13] See Mediawatch Uk for more information. http://www.mediawatchuk.com/our-history/

Declarations:

> **"On that day the deaf will hear the words of a book, And out of their gloom and darkness the eyes of the blind will see [the words of the book]"** Isaiah 29:18 (Amplified).

> **"We give thanks and all the praise and glory that you teach us to follow the narrow path that leads to the Highway of Holiness"** Isaiah 35:8 (Amplified).

For Your Word never returns void.

Desensitization

Media is being used like an intravenous line to anaesthetize people into a spiritual numbness. We can get swept away with bold and subliminal messages alike, with images, sounds, and smells that adversely affect us without us even realizing it and then, all of a sudden, we are caught unaware, denounce the hand of the potter, and masquerade in false images, as it is written in Isaiah 29:16.

Forgiveness: Lord God, forgive us for our slumbering, for not having stayed awake and alert. For allowing ourselves to be seduced, knowing that it only takes one bite to become hooked, numbing our senses, so we are rendered paralysed.

Declarations: We declare that we are appointed watchmen for this hour. We will keep watching and praying that we may not submit to temptation. We are dressed in readiness and prudent with our lamps full of oil, fully aware that the day of the Lord will come like a thief in the night.

Prayer for Overcoming the Media King

We ask you, Lord Jesus, for forgiveness for us and on behalf of others. We pray for the healing of Great Britain and deliverance from the consequences of following the false god that is the media. By the precious blood of Jesus, we are all washed and made clean.

With the Sword of the Spirit, we chop the head off the Apollyon, the king of media, and stake the ground, taking possession of this land. We act in the authority given to us by Almighty God and take dominion over the enemy and its spoils, replenishing all that was stolen.

> **"who gave Himself [as a sacrifice to atone] for our sins [to save and sanctify us] so that He might rescue us from this present evil [a]age, in accordance with the will and purpose and plan of our God and Father"** Galatians 1:4 (Amplified).

49

On June 16th, two days before the prayer summit, LBC Radio reported from the national news that Jo Cox, the British Labour Party Member of Parliament for Batley and Spen, was shot and stabbed multiple times in Birstall, West Yorkshire, shortly before she was due to hold a constituency surgery. A 52-year-old local man, Thomas Mair, was arrested for killing Cox and was subsequently charged with her murder and other offences.

At the prayer summit, the Lord also led us to repent for Jo Cox's murder and appropriate the blood of Jesus over it to prevent the enemy from using the incident to sabotage the Lord's plans. (People who wanted Great Britain to remain within the EU blamed the EU Referendum Campaign for her murder and were pressuring the government to cancel the planned EU Vote).

The day after the prayer summit, on June 19th, I listened to Ukip leader Nigel Farage on LBC Radio suggesting that "the tragedy of the murder of Labour MP Jo Cox has taken some of the momentum out of the campaign to get Britain out of the European Union." However, we knew that the Lord had the final say. We knew that the unfortunate event which the remain campaign was seeking to use as a distraction would not cripple the nation from making the right decision in how to vote.

PRAYER SKYPE

As I recalled David Cameron's speech in which he gave Great Britain the mandate to decide whether to remain in the EU or leave the EU, I suddenly perceived that the Lord had appointed him as the Prime Minister for that one specific purpose.

On the surface, the body of Christ did not have a voice throughout the campaign, as the leading campaigners sought expert opinions and leant on their own understandings for direction. However, there was a remnant of the body of Christ rising across Great Britain, fervently seeking God's intervention and direction, which would later turn the tide of the country. For our part, the Great Britain prayer court met on Skype to intercede once a week.

A week before voting day on June 23rd, the Lord had laid it on my heart for us to increase our weekly midnight prayer Skype to daily, right up until the close of the voting day, to legislate and decree the Lord's plans to prevail over the direction of the vote.

Throughout that time, the Lord filled us with revelation and confirmation of His will. For example, Miss P shared this with us. The first thing I want to tell you is that I was very much against Brexit because:

1. I thought the unity of Europe was better than division, and, as David Cameron said, "Together is better during the remain campaign leading up the EU Referendum vote." I totally agreed with that.

2. As an Italian living in Great Britain and without a proper permanent job, I thought Brexit would be a big complication of my life and of the lives of many Europeans living in the country, so I said, "No, thanks."

However, after lifting this all up to God in prayer, I completely changed my mind as God showed me HIS point of view, which was very different from mine!

The first picture I received was a vision of a huge blue carpet with stars all around (that's the symbol of the EU) and in the middle of the EU carpet, I saw the statue of Satan, the one with a human body and a goat head! God clearly showed me that the EU leadership with headquarters in Brussels, Belgium, is evil, not Christian at all, and their motives and purposes are satanic. It is all anti-Christian, pro-multi-faith, pro-new world order, freemasonry, and occultist staff!! If we chose to stay in the EU, we would also have chosen to stay under their leadership and rules, and God was NOT happy with that.

Then I had a second picture, in which the EU was like a nicely decorated vase. It looked attractive, but it was deceptive. In reality, it was not a good thing at all. The vase represented control, oppression, limitation, and lack of freedom (which came from the EU headquarters and leadership). Then I saw God breaking the vase with a hammer because the EU is NOT of or from Him. It is a political agreement made by people who follow their own interests, not God's. Then, with the dust that comes out of the broken vase, God builds a new thing and a new shape for Great Britain.

So, the vase was meant to be broken first, to see a new thing coming out of it.

I believe there will be other countries leaving the EU (a strong conviction that I have in my heart).

After sharing my visions with other prophetic Christians, I have been advised to watch David Hathaway's documentary on YouTube called, "The Rape of Europe." Shared Miss P, one of our intercessors

I remember Mrs O (an intercessor from my local church, the Commonwealth Community Fellowship [CCF]), sharing with me a few days before the vote that after praying one day, she went to the bathroom and felt a stirring in her spirit, so she went back to kneel and pray. As she felt the Holy Spirit moving, she asked the Lord, "What does this mean?" She said she heard Him say that "This is victory." She then said that "On the tube going to work, as I passed to get onto the Piccadilly line platform, there was an advertisement on the wall and in big letters was the word VICTORY."

Mr. G, another intercessor on our team, reported that while at the movie theater a couple of months prior, he saw an advertisement for the forthcoming movie, "Independence Day," which would open in theaters nationwide on June 23rd, and wondered why the movie producers chose such a seemingly insignificant date for its opening, rather than July 4th, American Independence Day. He went on to say that on his way back home at 9pm from praying at Parliament Square with a bunch of other believers, he again saw an advertisement for the movie "Independence Day," only this time the ad was displayed on a bus. He again wondered why they were promoting the movie's opening on the 23rd and said that the Lord impressed on his heart that it was because "The United State of America's Independence Day is the 4th of July and the 23rd would be recorded as Great Britain's Independence Day"

Following on from midnight Skype prayer leading into the 23rd, Mrs D (the prayer team leader in my church) said she asked the Lord for a sign and decided to look out of her window and saw lightening in the sky. The nation experienced the reality of the song "Let the Heavens Open Up like Rain" as a thunderstorm, during which heavy rain fell for the whole day.

THE TIMES

THURSDAY JUNE 23 2016 | THE TIMES.CO.UK | NO 71944

£1.40

MAX 22 MIN 46

REFERENDUM SPECIAL

DAY OF RECKONING

Remain a member of
the European Union

Leave the
European Union

EU REFERENDUM VOTING DAY

We continued to pray fervently on Skype at 10:00 p.m. on voting day until the very end at 6:30 a.m. on Thursday, June 24th, 2016, when the vote count was completed and the results were published online. We had literally engaged in spiritual warfare the whole time, so we were so elevated with joy at the Brexit results that instead of being tired for lack of sleep, we were full of energy and excitement as each one of us went off to get ready to go to work. Some of the news headlines on the Brexit results included the following:

The Aftermath of Brexit Voting Day

"We have done it! 'Independence Day'! Today is a victory for decent, ordinary people who have taken on the establishment and won," reported Nigel Farage the following day on the national news. **(Remember Mr J's word of knowledge about our Independence Day)**

National Quotes from the Church

The man who led the pro-EU group, Christians for Europe, Michael Sadgrove, said he was *"heartbroken"* and it was a *"terrible day for Britain."* **Premier Christian Radio**

The Church of England's Bishop in Europe, the Rotary (Rt.) Rev. Robert Innes said that the vote had been a failure of political leadership and a *"squandering of the birth-right of our young people."* **Telegraph, 9 July 2016**

As I listened to the people's lack of gratitude, I wept before the Lord and cried out for mercy, rather than judgement, to prevail over Great Britain. At that moment, the Lord helped me to see the parallel of the exodus of the Israelites from the bondage and affliction from Egypt to Britain's Brexit from the EU. Despite God's divine intervention and the signs and wonders He displayed in setting the Israelites free from captivity, when the Israelites started to crave for meat and bread, they began to murmur and complain against God that they were better off in bondage in Egypt, where they had food, rather than facing the uncertainty ahead of them and trusting the Lord for provision as they journeyed through the wilderness to get to the promised land of Canaan filled with milk and honey. As I pondered on this, I asked the Lord what we. as spiritual watchmen and intercessors, should do next, as I knew that we had to do something quick to reinforce our victory in the natural realm, for this was a spiritual battle, also, not merely a natural one. To see God's plans fulfilled, I perceived that we needed to agree with the things on His heart for Great Britain through prayer and intercession. It was at that moment that the Lord impressed on me to mobilise prayer for forty days at Parliament Square.

Meanwhile, millions of Remainers started a petition asking the government for a second referendum, David Cameron resigned as Prime Minister, and there was division within the government and amongst politicians.

"I was absolutely clear about my belief that Britain is stronger, safer and better off inside the EU. I made clear the referendum was about this, and this alone, not the future of any single politician, including myself. But the British people made a different decision to take a different path. As such, I think the country requires fresh leadership to take it in this direction," David Cameron said on a national news broadcast.

THE TIMES

SATURDAY

June 25 2016 | thetimes.co.uk | No 71946

Weekend Newspaper of the Year

 Max 21C min 4C

Only
£1.50

The end is nigh:
David Cameron
with his wife,
Samantha, on his
way to resign

Brexit earthquake

● Prime minister announces resignation ● Vote to leave threatens break-up of UK

Francis Elliott Political Editor
Sam Coates Deputy Political Editor

Brexit shock waves shook Britain to its core yesterday, forcing David Cameron to resign, causing a slump in global markets and heralding a break-up of the United Kingdom.

The country embarked on its new course with the leadership of both Westminster parties in peril. Boris Johnson is the frontrunner to become the next Tory leader and prime minister but Mr Cameron's allies swung behind Theresa May, the home secretary, as the best candidate to oppose him.

Labour MPs launched a coup against Jeremy Corbyn amid claims that his office had sabotaged the party's campaign to keep Britain in the European Union.

The pound touched a 31-year low and the FTSE 100 index tumbled 8.7 per cent after the country's exit was announced as dawn broke yesterday, though it later rallied. There were fears of falling house prices while economic forecasters downgraded Britain's growth prospects and its AAA credit rating came under threat.

Nicola Sturgeon, Scotland's first minister, served notice that she was

"highly likely" to fulfil her manifesto promise to hold another independence referendum because Scotland voted in favour of Remain by 62 per cent to 38 per cent. Across the UK, 51.9 per cent (17.4 million people) voted to leave the EU compared with 48.1 per cent (16.1 million) who wanted to stay.

The result, which most pollsters, bookmakers and markets had failed to predict, was put down in part to a high turnout of 72.2 per cent and strong Brexit support in the north of England and the Midlands. There was a stark generational divide, with three quarters of under-25s backing Remain. Experts

suggested that those who considered themselves to be the losers of globalisation had backed Brexit.

A stunned Brussels demanded that Britain start talks to leave the EU immediately. There were also calls from populist movements for similar referendums in France, Italy, the Netherlands and Denmark.

Standing with his wife, Samantha, outside Downing Street, Mr Cameron defended his decision to hold the poll and promised to respect the outcome. "I will do everything I can as prime minister to steady the ship over the coming weeks and months. But I do not think it

would be right for me to try to be the captain that steers our country to its next destination," he said.

Appearing close to tears, he finished by saying: "I love this country and I feel honoured to have served it and I will do everything I can in future to help this great country succeed."

Mr Cameron said that he wanted to have a new leader in place by the start of the Conservative Party conference in October. Tory MPs warned that he might have to stay longer in No 10 to allow for a longer contest.

Mr Johnson and Michael Gove, who
Continued on page 3, col 1

COMPREHENSIVE NEWS AND ANALYSIS

Blow to industry

Fears have increased that carmakers based in Britain and big aerospace companies such as Rolls-Royce and Airbus will move to transfer work abroad. **Page 8**

Matthew Parris

Our experiment in direct democracy is hurtling towards our tradition of representative democracy like some giant asteroid towards a moon. **Page 27**

Gibraltar claim

Spain reignited a diplomatic row with Britain when it said that the referendum had brought forward the day when a Spanish flag would fly over Gibraltar. **Pages 10-11**

Trump praises vote

Donald Trump, the Republican US presidential candidate, hailed the "amazing" result while visiting Scotland for the reopening of his golf resort. **Pages 14-15**

Tim Montgomerie

Dear Britain: Relax. Nigel Farage is not going to have substantial power in the new era, but he deserves credit for this exercise in democracy taking place at all. **Page 32**

Forty Days of Prayer at Parliament Square

On Saturday morning, June 26th, following the Brexit vote, I thought about the travel cost, time, and commitment that it would take. My 15-year-old son is in a full-time football program, so he only comes home on weekends and my 22-year-old daughter is independent. I get off work at 5:00 p.m. each day, so I had no excuse. I had a sense that this was one of my life assignments, so I resolved to obey and please God at all costs.

I had never led forty days' prayer before and never been to Parliament Square. I worked full-time as a Field Sales Executive in a very high-pressure environment and I was a single mother of two, but I had a sense of peace and a resolve to obey the Lord because the burden on my heart was heavy and saying yes to the Lord gave me relief from the burden. Still tearful, I got on the phone to share with some of the intercessors what the Lord had laid on my heart and they all agreed and said that they would support me in the forty-day assignment to Parliament Square.

From despair and sadness, I was suddenly filled with excitement, hope, and adventure as I perceived that the Lord was orchestrating watchmen to pray for Him to align and lead the UK to its prophetic destiny as a sheep nation from the EU. I resolved in my heart that regardless of how many people turned up to pray, I would, in obedience to the Lord, go to Parliament Square for the next forty days and pray as the Lord would lead me. So, I prayerfully put my trust and confidence in the Lord to stir up the hearts of the right intercessors to join me each day (see Jeremiah 17:7).

In the Bible, the Lord stirred up a remnant of able-bodied warriors to go to battle with Gideon when he went to fight against the enemies. So, I knew that what mattered was that I was joined by the right intercessors, with the same spirit and heart to join me each day at Parliament Square to pray and that is wasn't an issue of how many people turned up to pray.

I had never been to Parliament Square before, so I wasn't sure what to expect regarding the logistics or how many intercessors would turn up to intercede with me out of the ninety people whom I emailed on my mailing list. In my heart, I resolved that my role was to turn up and it was for the Lord to stir up the right people to join me.

In the following pages are extracts from emails I sent to Intercessors who joined me in prayer during the 40 days period.

Day 1: June 25, 2016:

Call to Action

Praise Father God, Who, in His great love for Great Britain, gave us mighty deliverance from our slavery to the EU yesterday.

> **"This is the [remarkable degree of] confidence which we [as believers are entitled to] have before Him: that [a]if we ask anything according to His will, [that is, consistent with His plan and purpose] He hears us"** 1 John 5:14 (Amplified).

Please prayerfully read through this whole email as there is an urgent call to action at the end!

1. Confirmation and Encouragement

June 18th: The Lord said that our intercession at the EU Summit would be used to turn the evil tide over society.

June 21st: Mrs O shared with me that after praying, she went to the bathroom and felt a stirring in her spirit, so she went back to kneel and pray. She felt the Holy Spirit moving, so she asked the Lord what does this mean? She said she heard, "This is Victory." Then she said, "On the tube going to work, as I passed to get onto the Piccadilly line platform, there was an advertisement on the wall and in big letters was the word 'VICTORY'."

June 22nd: Mr. J, another of our intercessors, reported that while at the movie theater a couple of months prior, he saw an advertisement for the forthcoming movie "Independence Day" that would open in theaters on June 23rd and wondered why the movie producers chose such a seemingly insignificant date for its opening, rather than July 4th, the date on which America obtained their independence? He went on to say that on his way back home at 9:00 p.m. from praying at Parliament Square with many other believers, he saw an advertisement for the movie again, this time on a bus, and again wondered why it was opening on June 23rd and said that the Lord impressed on his heart that it was because June 23rd would be Great Britain's independence day. America's is July 4th.

June 22nd: Following midnight prayer Skype leading into June 23rd, Mrs D said that she asked the Lord for a sign and when she looked out her window, she saw lightening in the sky.

2. Great Britain's Response

Like the Israelite's rescued from captivity, rather than rejoicing and thanking the Lord, the cry of the majority of the British people was murmuring, dismay, anger, fear, hatred, discord, and uncertainty because:

- A petition was circulating that was requesting a second referendum to overturn our victory.

- Our Prime Minister had resigned.

- There was division among the politicians.

- There was also division among the body of Christ, as many believers do not perceive what the Lord is doing in Great Britain right now.

3. It is Time for the Body of Christ to Awaken and Rise Up

The Lord is calling us to prayer and intercession to reinforce the victory that has been won. For forty days, beginning today, I am appealing to you to please join me in standing in the gap: (Excerpt from email I sent to intercessors)

- 8:00 p.m. tonight, at Parliament Square, meet at Jo Cox shrine

I know that this is a sacrifice, but this is a war! We are contending for the soul of our nation. Thank you so much for reading this, for your prayers and loving hearts for the Father, Great Britain, and to see the Lord's Kingdom established on earth in our nation as in Heaven.

"and My people, who are called by My Name, humble themselves, and pray and seek (crave, require as a necessity) My face and turn from their wicked ways, then I will hear [them] from heaven, and forgive their sin and heal their land." 2 Chronicles 7:14 (Amplified).

PLEASE RSVP ME!! Praying on. Yours in the Lord. YO Cedar

Day 2: June 26, 2016:

Thank you for the amazing warriors who joined me last night and for the emails of encouragement that I received. The Lord is preparing the body of Christ for the end-time harvest. He is getting the foundation right, including repentance, awakening, revelation of the Fatherhood of God, and true identities are being restored.

Ten of us met from 8:00 p.m. to 10:00 p.m. to worship and enthrone the King of Kings over our nation, and to repent and ask the Lord to realign the church with its first love and Kingdom purpose (see Revelation 2:4).

When Big Ben started to chime at 10:00 p.m., Alice said she had a sense that the Lord intended us to linger until that time. So, what is the biblical significance of ten? Law, government order and obligation, responsibilities, pastor, testing, trials. The Lord had strategically placed us at Parliament Square to enforce our Kingdom authority over the government and to pray for endurance and mercy as the nation transitions.

Why Would the Lord Have Watchmen Pray at Trafalgar Square for Forty Days? To Overrule the Spirit of Discord, Unbelief, Pain, and Turmoil Spreading Across Great Britain

- Forty generally symbolises a period of testing, trial, or probation.

- The number forty can also represent a generation of man (because of the Israelites' sins after leaving Egypt).

- Due to the Israelites' unbelief and rebellion, it took them forty years, rather than forty days, to reach the promised land.

- Moses was on Mount Sinai for forty days and nights as he received the love letter from God. He also sent spies, for forty days, to investigate the land God promised the Israelites as an inheritance (see **Numbers 13:2**)

- The prophet Jonah powerfully warned ancient Nineveh, for forty days, that its destruction would come because of its many sins (see **Jonah 3:4**).

- Elijah went forty days without food or water at Mount Horeb.

- Jesus was tempted by the devil not just three times, but MANY times during the forty days and nights He fasted just before His ministry began. He also appeared to His disciples and others for forty days after His resurrection from the dead.

Why Parliament Square?

- Parliament Square is a square at the north-west end of the Palace of Westminster in London. It features a large open green area in the centre with trees to its west and contains ten statues of statesmen and other notable individuals.

- As well as being one of London's main tourist attractions, it is also the place where many demonstrations and protests have been held. The square is overlooked by various official buildings, including legislature to the east (in the Houses of Parliament), executive offices to the north (on Whitehall), the judiciary to the west (the Supreme Court), and the church to the south (with Westminster Abbey).

- We repented on behalf of the body of Christ for the murmuring and complaining like the Israelites did when the Lord delivered them out of Egypt. We also asked that Father God's mercy prevails over judgment.

- We cried out for the spirit of discernment and intimacy with Father God to be restored so that eyes and ears perceive what the Lord is doing. We want to partner with what the Lord is doing, rather than fight against it.

- Great Britain is crying out for guidance and direction, providing the body of Christ with a great opportunity to show non-Christians the way.

- We declared that the doors the Lord opens, no man can shut. The doors that He shuts, no man can open. We came against a U-turn from our decision to Brexit. The UK is separated from ungodly alliances (spirit of Babel and control) to align with Israel, according to the Lord's will, but also to align with the Lord's purpose and destiny for Great Britain.

- We prayed for the Josephs, Nehemiah's, Esther's, and people like Naaman's servant to awaken, for believers in seemingly insignificant jobs who have access to people of influence to awaken to their assignments of praying and giving words of wisdom to influencers in parliament.

Day 3: JUNE 27, 2016:

Thank you so much to those warriors who've joined us in prayer at Parliament Square and to those who are praying alongside us, with and for us. Each prayer day has been unique and awesome! "'[a]Your kingdom come, Your will be done On earth as it is in heaven" Mathew 6:10 (Amplified)

There is so much that I would like to share with you, but time will not permit me at this moment. You know the song that we sing in church, "There's an Army Rising Up?" Well, it's happening right now, right before our eyes. The army of the Lord (the body of Christ) is awakening to its true identity and calling to advance His Kingdom in Great Britain. Praise Abba Father for His loving kindness and mercies toward us!

Parliament Square: Weekly Updates

I am very sorry, but due to the current lack of manpower, I will be providing you updates once a week, rather than daily, to share testimonies for encouragement and to give you tools to help you pray more strategically for the healing and reformation of our nation. You will receive the first update by the end of the day on Friday.

Help Needed, Please!

Meanwhile, to praise God and give Him all the glory, the Ekklesia Church has mobilised their members to come join us in prayer once a week. If you can, please also help mobilise support from your church and fellow intercessors to commit to joining us one or more days during the forty days of prayer court at Parliament Square.

Forthcoming Prayer Walk Assignments for Your Diary

1. Creativity Gate: Soho Prayer Walk, 10:00 p.m. this Friday

2. The Lord wants to redeem and restore creativity gate. If you are creative or have a passion for creativity, arts, or entertainment, etc., then please RSVP and join us. (If you can, please pray and fast that day.)

Economics Gate: Stock Exchange Prayer Walk, 10:00 p.m. – 12:00 a.m., Friday, July 8

In the midst of the huge economic shaking that Great Britain is currently facing, following our Brexit, it's timely to prayer walk at this gate and allow the Lord to restore and bring alignment to our finances. If you would like to join us, please RSVP ASAP. (If you can, please pray and fast that day.)

I love you with the love of Christ and thank God for you. May His blessings and Shalom overtake you beyond measure.

Day 4: June 28, 2016:

We initially met at the Square, then nine of us were led to hold prayer at the entrance of the Supreme Court:

- The Square is full of monuments of bold and courageous men who fought for the cause of justice. Father God, release that same spirit over the body of Christ, our politicians, and our nation.

- Father God so loves our nation. As we met to pray, David's Tent (DT) were holding a worship meeting a few blocks away. At the end of DT, one of the ladies with a guitar was heading home when she saw us praying and felt prompted to join us. She played her guitar and led us in singing "He Has Removed the Yoke" while we stood at the entrance of the Supreme Court.

- We asked the Lord to remove whoever needs to be removed from Parliament (those who will oppose His will and purposes) and appoint those whom He has handpicked (men/women with spirit of integrity, Kingdom minded, bold and courageous, who will stand for righteousness, despite opposition, just as King David, Abraham Lincoln, and William Wilberforce did).

- Supreme Court -- Repentance and redemption needed so that justice and righteousness are restored. The Lord establishes His rule and heavenly court. Dethrones all falsehood, and everything that stands against the true knowledge of Christ.

- There is a huge sense of the magnitude of orphans and spiritual orphans in our nation. Father God asking, "Whom can I send?"

Prayer

Father God, restore and bring wholeness to broken families. Hearts of parents turn to their children and those of children to their parents. Give the body of Christ the strategies to minister, love, affirm, and model Christ to dysfunctional families. Raise up spiritual fathers and mothers to counsel, adopt, mentor, befriend, and foster the orphans.

Father God, be enthroned at the Supreme Court and over our nation. His Word, His ways be adopted in our society.

Days 5 through 7: June 29 through July 1, 2016:

Five of us ("five" signifies God's mercies) started at Parliament Square, then we were prompted to go into Westminster Abbey during a vigil for the Battle of Somme.

Answered Prayer

- Praise God for answered prayer. At the eleventh hour, Michael Gove applied to run for Prime Minister, forcing Boris Johnson to drop out of the race.

- Nicola Sturgeon did not succeed with negotiations to separate Scotland from the rest of Great Britain. The EU will not have separate negotiations with Scotland, only with Great Britain as a nation.

- We praised Father God for the young men playing sports in the middle of the Square.

- We started out at the Square, and then the Lord prompted us to go and release His Word and speak the life of God into Westminster Abbey. We joined the long queue who were attending the night vigil for the service for the Battle of Somme. Strangely, the only sermon read at the Abbey were letters to the dead soldiers. There was no Bible reading (it's the Word of God that brings life and liberty) and there was no led prayer or praise and worship to Father God.

Headlines

Prayer

Father God, as You intervened in the appointment of King David by giving Samuel discernment and ears to hear, direct the hearts of the Conservative MPs to nominate the right two candidates to run for Prime Minister. Give voters discernment and pliable hearts so that they will not vote for the next PM in accordance with the flesh, but, rather, your promptings.

Father God, shake off falsehood, luke-warmness, deception, division, religious spirit, deafness, and spiritual blindness from the body of Christ. Cause the body of Christ to awaken to its true identity and calling in advancing Your Kingdom. (Pray especially for Westminster Abbey. Many come looking for hope but are presented with deadness of religion, a misrepresentation of Father God, Who is love, alive, and full of goodness.)

Father God, restore recreation, harmony, and community among the young and older people, alike. We rebuke the spirit of division, violence, fear, and hatred, releasing God's presence into our communities, His love to reign.

Father God, draw the hearts of the broken-hearted and lost to You in this hour. Position and align believers to share the Gospel, disciple, encourage, and bless wherever they go.

- In the midst of hatred, racism, fear, anxiety, and confusion, we declare emotional, mental, spiritual, and physical healing over Great Britain. May the precious love of God shake out everything contrary.

- As we prayed, suddenly we saw a huge, beautiful double rainbow enveloped over Parliament. We knew the Lord gave us this sign as encouragement of His faithfulness. His mercy prevail over judgement. May hope be restored to Great Britain.

- We declare that Father God reigns over Parliament, every government department, education, arts, and entertainment.

- We sensed that Scotland was in a lot of pain and felt a sense of betrayal. Prophetically, Jane, our Scottish intercessor, forgave Helen, our English intercessor, and repentance, healing, and love were restored.

- We declare healing over Scotland, and that its relationship with the rest of Great Britain, especially England, should be restored, as prophetic.

Prayer

Father God, break every ungodly alliance that Great Britain has in place. Father God, realign Great Britain with Israel.

Father God, shake off all that needs to be shaken off the body of Christ, including every wrinkle, every blemish, and cause us to become "Christ-like." The world recognises us by our fruits.

Father God, cause Your glory to so shine upon the body of Christ that those in darkness encounter Jesus and the good news everywhere we go.

Father God, cause Conservative MPs to select the two candidates whom You have handpicked. Give them discernment, ears to hear, and eyes to see. And when the vote opens to the conservative members, may their hearts be turned in the direction of Your will, voting for the new Leader of Conservatives, the Prime Minister whom You have handpicked before the foundation of the world, for this hour. Let this person possess integrity, conviction, godly values, wisdom, humility, and let him/her be Kingdom minded, as were Abraham Lincoln and William Wilberforce.

Soho: Redeeming Creativity Gate (10:00 p.m.)

The vibes at Soho were filled with community and creativity. We carried out prophetic acts, including using salt to restore purity, consecrate creative gate so that its content—entertainment, arts, etc.—were wholesome, edifying, and pure (e.g., "Lord of the Rings," tasteful fashion, etc.). As we were about to leave, we met a believer who worked for SALT TV at Soho, who asked us what we were doing carrying salt around. Awestruck, he took a photo of us. It was a divine moment of confirmation that the Lord was restoring creativity to the body of Christ.

- Repentance where the church, parents, teachers, and others have stifled creativity in children, youth, and adults.

- Repentance for the church not encouraging or supporting creatives.

- Repentance for lack of community among believers, as in the book of Acts (Jews and Muslims help each other develop businesses).

- We praised God for restoring truth to the body of Christ regarding their creativity.

- I saw a vision of stacks and stacks of creative gifts stacked up in white wrapped boxes waiting for believers to come and collect them. (Innovative, creative solutions to every problem plaguing society today.)

- I woke up this morning with a tangible creative idea from God. Don't be left out. Ask the Lord what innovation is available for you today. Claim yours from Father God today.

Days 8 through 14: July 2 through 8, 2016:

These past two weeks have been described as the most traumatic which Great Britain has faced since the last world war. However, in the midst of all the shaking and darkness, what has the Lord been doing? As we continue to hold prayer court at Parliament Square, it has become clear that the Lord desires that His mercy prevails over judgement. He is awakening the body of Christ to showcase His glory in unprecedented ways. Please see this week's updates below, answered prayers, direction, and wisdom which the Lord is imparting to the body of Christ to bring about revival and reformation.

A big thank you to the watchmen who have selflessly come to join us in releasing prophetic decrees at Parliament Square, as with Deborah, in the Bible. We meet at 8:00 p.m. daily at Parliament Square. Please join us in reshaping the history of Great Britain. For more frequent updates, please visit us on Facebook (https://www.facebook.com/britainprayercout/).

Day 8: July 2, 2016

Jealous for the Lord over the passion that Labour supporters displayed for Corbyn:

When we arrived to pray, I was amazed and jealous for the Lord by the thousands of Labour supporters who came in unity to Parliament Square to rally their support for Jeremy Corbyn, Leader of the Labour Party, in protest of the MPs who were putting pressure on him to step down from leadership.

"Thousands of people attended another rally in Parliament Square to express support for Corbyn. Organised by Momentum, the event took place at a meeting of the Parliamentary Labour Party and upheld a motion of no confidence against the party leader in the House of Commons.

The supporters came from different backgrounds (age, race, social class, religion, and gender), but were united in their passion and agenda as one. I thought about the body of Christ. How awesome it would be if we had a united voice to the government and the nation in this hour. That night, seven of us met (biblical meaning for "seven" is new beginnings).

We repented of all the murmuring, anger, and bitterness, and asked the Lord to awaken the body of Christ to its true identity and purpose of advancing His Kingdom. Ability to reflect the Father's heart to all those with whom we come in contact, releasing peace, love, hope, and encouragement to those in turmoil, facing hatred, discord, uncertainty, and despair. Father God, align the hearts of believers and the nation to your heartbeat so that they discern, comprehend, and cooperate with what You are doing in Great Britain.

- It was wonderful when a Jewish believer joined us in prayer. We repented for replacement theology that has become prominent in the body of Christ and anti-Semitism that has crept into our government, predominately the Labour Party. Revelation to be released to the body of Christ and our nation about our commission to align with and support Israel.

- We prayed that the 135 Christian MPs develop a deeper intimacy with God, and a revelation of their purpose at Parliament (e.g., William Wilberforce), that they will influence their peers with godliness and Kingdom strategies, that we create transformation in government.

- Two businessmen, one English and one Asian Hindu, came up to us for prayer. With gladness of heart, we prophesied and encouraged them both with the love of God.

Main Prayer Headlines:

Father God, awaken the body of Christ, for Great Britain is waiting for the manifestation of the Son's of God (see Romans 8:19).

Father God, tear down the walls of division among the body of Christ (see John 17:21).

Father God, restore wholeness to families, neighbourhoods, workplaces, and society (see John 10:10).

The love of God to move the body of Christ to disciple our nation. Fathers and spiritual fathers to adopt, foster, mentor, and befriend the orphans (see Mathew 28:19).

We came against Scotland breaking away from the UK. For the doors which the Lord opens, no man can shut, and the door which He shuts, no man can open (see Revelation 3:7).

Day 9: July 3, 2016: Spiritual Intensity at the heart of Parliament:

After being spiritually challenged by the labour support rally for Corbyn the day before, the Lord gave me great encouragement today because as I arrived, there was another group of intercessors from different churches praying in the centre of Parliament Square, the same spot occupied by the people rallying the day before. I was also amazed at Father God's precision in timing, as a group of Christians finished their session of prayer and worship right before our group commenced prayer at 8:00 p.m.

As we started to pray, we noticed lots of police turning up with their sirens blaring and wondered what was going on. Then another group of campaigners arrived on foot and in vehicles. They were very bitter and angry, hurling curses at our nation. We watched in shock as a van driving around the square with EU flags and posters with words mocking Great Britain, saying "Fool Great Britain."

At the same time, there was a great sense of community in the Square. Families and friends chilling out together. In the midst of recent traumatic events, this was clearly God's grace upon our nation. We acknowledged that in some countries, there would be political upheaval and violence, but during the national shakings, there was order, not anarchy.

- We prayed for wholeness and community to be restored to broken, dysfunctional, hurting families.

- God's intervention in appointing a new Prime Minister, a person with a pliable heart, like King David, and a person who is Kingdom minded, like William Wilberforce and Abraham Lincoln. Kingdom strategies that will bring reformation to education, government, media, arts and entertainment, economy, faith, and families.

- As we prayed, the Lord's revelation came to us, that as the body of Christ (His bride) rises up from complacency and luke-warmness, we become fervent in our love for Father God and His ways. We will live and act like Christ. Signs and wonders would accompany our works, causing government and society to seek godly counsel and direction on all the issues and problems facing society (e.g., Smith Wigglesworth didn't need to petition the government about alcohol; instead, his yielding to the Holy Spirit caused people to be so filled with the Holy Spirit that they turned away from pubs. Rather than seeking comfort from alcohol, they got comfort from the Lord. Pubs literally went out of business).

Prayer

For the body of Christ to come aflame with the love of God, and for fervent believers to rise up and come ablaze with flames of love, and flames of rivals dispelling darkness wherever they go.

Day 10: July 4, 2016:

- Father God, direct the MPs to vote a new Leader of Conservatives in accordance with Your will. Give them discernment and wisdom not to vote according to the flesh (selfish motivations or leaning on their own understanding). A Prime Minister with conviction, God fearing, integrity, Kingdom minded. Five Christian MPs are now running for the position of the new Leader of Conservatives / Prime Minister. A leader capable of leading the nation to its destiny purpose, following on from the Brexit.

- Song of Solomon declared over the body of Christ, intimacy with the Lord. MPs have spiritual encounters with Christ Jesus like Apostle Paul on the road to Damascus.

- Encounters like Wilberforce had (it changed his entire values and political career). Father God, give every MP access to spiritual mentors like Mordechai was to Esther, Samuel was to David, and John Newton was to Wilberforce.

Day 11: July 5, 2016:

- We walked past many media vans parked at Queen Elizabeth II Conference Building behind the Supreme Court, in readiness for the Chilcot Report findings to be presented tomorrow. We sensed that many a lot of people would be angered if justice and truth were not upheld, fueling even more dissatisfaction with government. We declared the Magna Carter (Great Britain was founded on Scripture) and prayed for John Chilcot to be filled with boldness and confidence, as was Daniel, in the Bible, to stand for truth, justice, and righteousness. Mercy in place of judgement for Tony Blair.

- Father God, cleanse this nation of every ungodliness. Take Your seat. of governance. Be enthroned over every sphere of society. Bring truth to spiritually dead churches, believers, and non-believers (e.g., Saul thought he was doing the work of God when persecuting and murdering believers until he met with Jesus and was converted, thereby becoming Paul).

Day 12: July 6, 2016:

- The nation was shocked by the Chilcot report. There was no whitewashing of facts. John Chilcot's reporting was described as careful, bold, precise, and full of truth and justice. Protestors outside the building had to put down their signs and go home.

- We praised God for answered prayers. We repented for an anti- Israeli march held last Sunday and for the negative spins published by the media, in particular, BBC.

- We declared that Great Britain would make the right alliances and cut off every ungodly alliance (e.g., false gods like Hindu [yoga event, etc., normalised in society, even in some churches).

- God, awaken the body of Christ. Tear down every wall, including religion, self-centeredness, deception, idolatry, disobedience, division, and being halfhearted. Awaken us to disciplining our nation.

Day 13: July 7, 2016:

- Conservative MPs narrowed to two female Christians from State Schools (one, a remainer and one, a Brexiter). Father God, cause the 150,000 conservative voters to vote according to Your promptings. Someone bold, confident, who stands for truth, conviction, and integrity. The wisdom of Solomon, and openness with his/her faith, as was Wilberforce.

- Discernment and wisdom to appoint the right cabinet members.

- Honour and respect restored to government, specifically regarding how Theresa May and Andrea Leadsom conduct their forthcoming campaigns.

- Father God, release a spirit of Jehu. Remove what needs to be removed in government, this nation, and the body of Christ. Every idol and cut off every ungodly alliance.

- Repentance where the church has turned its back against prophecy. Repentance where preachers have been afraid to preach the truth. Freedom and joy restored to the church. Ears to hear. Deliverance, inner healing. The message of repentance and true Gospel to be restored to churches.

Day 14: July 8, 2016:

We are in a time in which nothing is impossible. In the natural, two female Christians were nominated by conservative cabinet members to be the next Prime Minister. This is the time for the body of Christ to believe again. Awaken to their dreams and destiny callings. The Lord led Great Britain out of the EU, just as He led the Israelites out of Egypt. He has a great destiny and purpose for Great Britain. The doors which He shuts, no man can open.

We come against hidden agendas of the enemy (e.g., the division in the Labour Party; 300,000 are reported to have joined the party these past few days, majority to support the Leader, Jeremy Corbyn).

Father God, bring alignment and godly order to the Labour Party. Remove all falsehoods and make room for the leader/s whom You have appointed in this hour. Father God, expose all the enemy plans to undermine Your plans and purposes, not only in the Labour Party but also in all government member parties.

News reports indicate a 48 % rise in xenophobia and racism following the Brexit.

We declare the love of God shakes out insecurities, fears, and anxieties that cause people to display hatred toward others. Peace and honour be restored.

Father God, release angelic assignments to the body of Christ. Watchmen, awaken to prayer in every church.

- Discernment to stop the enemy from causing a U-turn back to aligning with the EU.

- We declared Psalm 29 over Great Britain.

Day 15: July 9, 2016:

We got on our knees, praying for men. Freedom for them to rise up in their role of kings and priests. We came against the spirit of Jezebel and religion plaguing the body of Christ.

- Father God, reveal why men are not stepping up.

- Salvation Army Conference. Seemingly ignorant of everything that's happened around them. A reflection of the body of Christ. Father God, awaken the body of Christ to its true Identities and eyes to see. Ears to hear the times that we are in. In the midst of darkness, lead people to see that Your Word is still relevant today and that the Earth is awaiting the manifestation of the Son of God.

- Media: Spin on Andrea Leadsom. That true, pure media would be upheld. Voters to be discerning and not influenced by the media, but by hearts directed by the Lord in the direction to vote for the next Prime Minister.

- Wisdom and discretion added to Andrea Leadsom. Honouring and respect upheld in government and the way that women running for office carry out their campaigns to be elected as Prime Minister.

- Amazed by the spirit of dedication and selflessness of the Cancer Walk rally organisers. Prayed for a commitment like that to be evident in the body of Christ. Jesus movement.

We declared Galatians 3.

Day 16: July 10, 2016 (see Psalms 105, Romans 8, and Revelation 3):

We declared a spirit of awakening. Refining. Shedding of the worthless and being forced from a place or position.

Meanwhile, Andrea Leadsom got in trouble for an inappropriate comment about Theresa May's inability to have children this week. It was reported that twenty MPs said they would resign if she was elected Prime Minister.

Prompted by the Holy Spirit, a lady named Esther came to join us. This directed us to pray for the Holy Spirit to impart to the new Prime Minister a pliable heart, wisdom, discretion, knowing when to speak, how to speak, a spirit of conviction, boldness, and confidence. Preferential treatment like Esther imparted to the woman whom the Lord has ordained to be the new Prime Minister. We prayed that the vote would carry overwhelming distinction to the right candidate and be a vote that cannot be disputed.

For the new Prime Minister to have the wisdom of Solomon to appoint the right cabinet ministers. Select by the Lord, not by human understanding. Men of excellent spirits like Joseph, conviction, integrity, and highly skilled.

Alignment with Israel. The body of Christ to rise up.

Revelation shared by Erica, an intercessor while we were praying together: "There was a great table that had paint and varnish on it. It was then stripped from all its paint and varnish so that all that remained was bare wood. In the same manner, Father God is going to strip the country so that it can be brought back to its Judeo -Christian roots."

Day 17: July 11, 2016 – Suddenlys:

Andrea Leadsom apologised to Theresa May for her comment on her not being able to have children. Consequently, she dropped out of the race for Prime Minister, stating that she wanted to avoid division within her party and put the needs of the country first. (MPs favoured Theresa May, but Party Members favoured Andrea Leadsom). The media and nation later commended Andrea Leadsom for her dignity and honourable action of stepping down.

Theresa May was elected as the next Prime Minister. David Cameron said that she would be in office by Wednesday night. We praised God for this "suddenly" and acceleration, as Cameron had previously said that the new Prime Minister would be in office on September 9th.

Theresa May said she was humbled and delighted to have been chosen as the next Prime Minister.

Angela Eagle officially launched her campaign to run against Corbyn as Leader of the Labour Party.

We again prayed for the Lord to bring order and align Great Britain with the Labour Party. For whatever and whoever should be removed to be removed. Plans of the enemy to use the division in the Labour Party to undermine what the Lord is unleashing in Great Britain and to bring our nation to defeat.

We also came against petitions and rallies seeking to undermine the overall decision for the nation to Brexit. We asked that the body of Christ would have the same passion and tenacity in standing for truth, righteousness, and justice, thereby advancing the Lord's Kingdom.

Jonathan led two young men on vacation from Europe to Christ in the Square.

Day 18: July 12, 2016:

Father God, we call forth a Caleb anointing to come upon the Labour Party as Shadow Cabinet to sharpen and challenge and hold the government accountable for its actions.

Father God will call forth a spirit of unity and order into the Labour Party.

Father God, You have called us, our nation, to realign with Israel. Please put it in the Queen and Prince Philip's (her husband's) hearts to visit Israel.

Father God, we thank You that Great Britain will honour the Balfour Treaty, which will be honoured by our new Government and Queen by the power of Your might.

Day 19: July 13, 2016 -- Appointment of New Prime Minister:

- Awakening and refining of the body of Christ. True knowledge of Father God. Clothed in the Lord's glory. Forgiveness where the body of Christ has misrepresented Christ to the larger society. Mantle of Esther, Joseph's anointing released to the body of Christ. Ability to know how and ability to truly reflect Jesus wherever we go.

- Caleb anointing released to the Labour Party. They will be united, full of conviction, integrity, and sharpen and challenge the Conservatives to do good.

- We pray for an open door for the Queen and her husband to visit Israel. We declare reconciliation and alignment. For the Balfour Treaty to be fully honoured.

- For a new government to favour Israel, restitution to Israel. Policies that support and favour Israel. Opening doors of blessings to Great Britain.

- We thanked the Lord for Boris's humility for accepting the position of Foreign Secretary and the Prime Minister for putting differences aside and honouring him with the opportunity. We also thanked the Lord for Amber Rudd, Philip Hammond, and the other newly appointed cabinet members.

- We continue to pray that they are filled with a spirit of excellence, godly wisdom, conviction, truth, and integrity. Anointing to lead our nation into its God-given destiny and purpose following the Brexit

- We prayed for the spirit of adoption to be released over our nation.

- For the Queen to commission Theresa May to form a new government.

- For a spirit of forgiveness between Boris and Gove.

- Thank You, Lord, for healing the economy. (It is getting better following the election of the new Prime Minister.

Day 20: July 14, 2016 -- Cabinet Reshuffle: Nation Shocked by the Major Reshuffling:

- We asked for revolution and shaking up of the media, for truth and integrity to be restored.

- We thanked the Lord for removing those who needed to be removed and for the appointment of a new cabinet (mainly from state schools, humble beginnings).

- Falsehood to be removed from the Labour Party.

- Prayed for the new cabinet ministers to be filled with the wisdom of Solomon, conviction, truth, integrity, boldness, and confidence, like Daniel. Pliable heart and humility, like David.

- Cabinet Ministers to be open about their Christian faith, like Wilberforce, and to be surrounded with godly counsel and spiritual mentors, like Esther, Wilberforce, and David.

- For the Prime Minister, her cabinet, and government to develop an intimacy with Father God. Favour and good success with trading and business agreements.

- For hope to form over Great Britain, and for the Lord to restore hope to the nation, hope in the new government, and to take Great Britain through a transition.

- For England, Scotland, Ireland, and its Isles to be aligned in unity. We came against Scotland's rebellion in wanting to undermine the nation's decision to Brexit.

- Repentance, forgiveness, and healing over Stephen Crabb's marriage. Humility and grace for him to deal with the sexting issue in a godly way that would glorify the Lord and minister to the public.

- Government ministers to be undergirded by prayer and godly counsel, and to encounter the Lord Jesus.

- Repentance over the role that England played against Scotland. Favour for the Prime Minister's meeting with Nicola Sturgeon tomorrow.

  - For the body of Christ to awaken and rise from religious mindsets, half-heartedness, and the spirit of slumber to their true identities in Christ, and for hearts to be ablaze for the Lord and see His Kingdom established in every gate of society (see dream from Ian, below).

  - Christian men (probably white and European) were running up wet mud tracks in a jungle setting to a meeting place, a wooden shack. As we reached the buildings, showers of arrows came raining down. I held up a board (or a shield) to fend off the arrows, but couldn't see anybody else do the same. When we were inside the building, I saw Christian men with sharpened wood sticks in their hands. They weren't very physically strong and were running around in confusion. I shouted out, "Where are your weapons? Where are your weapons?" Our enemies kept on appearing behind our backs. They were very strong, well-built, and had light-brown skin. They had a distinctive Mohican haircut and were very menacing, intent on killing us. They just kept on appearing behind our backs. The dream finished. We declared Ephesians 6 over the body of Christ.

  - We ministered to a young man today. Thank You, Lord, for the harvest is ripe. May we always be willing to share the Good News wherever we are.

Days 21 through 29: July 15 through 23, 2016:

  - The Prime Minister and Nicola Sturgeon meet to discuss the EU.

  - Nice: 84 dead in a terrorist attack.

- The Prime Minister is pressured by the Muslim community to legalise sharia courts.

We were led to hold prayer outside the Supreme Court and declared Romans 13 and Isaiah 42.

- We prayed for France and the Lord's divine intervention. For the nation to seek the Lord's face. For Kingdom strategies to eradicate terrorist attacks, as this was the fourth one. For Father God to reveal Himself to France, and for its broken-hearted people, and those in mourning to seek Him for deliverance and healing.

- For the body of Christ in France to awaken and contend for the soul of their nation.

- We declared that enough is enough with the compromise with the spirit of Islam being given permission to have a place in the UK. The Prime Minister will judge according to God's ways and have the wisdom from above, confidence and boldness to take a stand against sharia courts being given the legal ground that they are seeking in this nation. We declare that the law of this land aligns with righteousness, justice, and truth. The Lord eradicates anything contrary.

- For the body of Christ and this nation to become so ablaze with the love of God and the knowledge of Him that signs and wonders are manifested among us. For mosques to empty and for people to forsake their idols and turn to Christ

- We declare that Boris Johnson will be filled with the spirit of wisdom and truth during his timely appointment to France. He will strengthen our relationship with France and bring encouragement and hope. For the Lord's hand upon Boris to be so evident that the nation(s) recognise it and silence the critics as we prayed, Abi saw Boris wearing a hat).

- We declare that the Prime Minister and her cabinet, who have been appointed by the Lord, will be filled with divine wisdom, be firm in their decisions, bold, confident, Kingdom-minded, God pleasers, not man pleasers. For Kingdom strategies and favour to navigate Great Britain out of the EU, in alignment with the Lord's timeline and order.

- For the Lord to fill the new cabinet with the spirit of humility, putting the nation before their own personal agendas, and for them to not be complacent and be aware that their positions were by divine appointment and that they can be removed from their position at any time.

- We asked the Lord to expose all that is hidden and help us pray for His will regarding the stronghold of Islam and increase in secularism in Great Britain.

- As we prayed for favor and divine intervention in the meeting between the Prime Minister and Nicolas Sturgeon, it was impressed upon Rachel's heart to share the nursery rhyme about the lion (representing England) and the unicorn (representing Scotland). We soon found out that the union icon representing Scotland is paganist and has links to the Babel Spirit, thus explaining why the majority of Scotland voted to remain.

Cleansing Our Land: Preparation for Revival and Reformation:

We closed with a sense that the Lord wanted to cleanse our nation of everything that defiles it. In the past, we've had revivals, but they never lasted and communities often ended up worse off afterwards, as believers weren't exposed to the truth about advancing the Lord's Kingdom here on Earth and walking and operating in Kingdom authority. This is an area we all need to pray about, as the foundation of our nation is diluted with the Babel spirit.

*** Link to "The Mystical Unicorn of Scotland":
http://www.scottish-at-heart.com/unicorn-of-scotland.html ***

*** Link to the Royal Family Coat of Arms:
http://britishroyalfamily.com/royal-coat-of-arms/ ***

Please use these as a tool to pray for Great Britain. Hope you can join us to pray at 8:00 p.m. at Parliament Square.

Please forgive me for the delay in sending you this update. I have summarised the information contained herein to make it easier to read and pray through.

The underlining issues which the Lord has highlighted are that He wants to heal the land, so we must get rid of and repent of everything that defiles the land. Most importantly, He wants us to choose Him as our first love. As we enthrone Him and come into alignment with our true identities as ambassadors for Christ right here on Earth, we will see the transformation of society that we seek. For the evil that seems to prevail is a consequence of our own half-heartedness. I pray that the Holy Spirit sheds light to you as you read these.

The emphasis for This Week:

- We were reminded of the double rainbow over Parliament on July 1st. God is a covenant-keeping God and will keep His covenant with this nation. (See book front cover image)

- We praised and thanked Him for His mercy and protection in foiling terrorist attacks like the Army Officer who was nearly ambushed with a knife.

- We thanked Him for a new cabinet mantled with Joseph's anointing, restoring hope to the nation. Despite the shake up, there is no anarchy.

- We thanked the Lord for exposing all the ploys of the enemy. He reveals to redeem.

- We thanked the Lord for the full moon right next to Parliament. His wonders are so evident over our nation. May eyes be opened to the truth of how great and awesome God is!

Healing our Land: repentance for idolatry, religious spirits, ungodly laws, compromise, family breakdowns and dysfunctions, and luke-warmness in the body of Christ

Deliverance from the stronghold of Islam: The Lord exposed the spirit behind it and gave our government the boldness to renounce it.

The body of Christ must reawaken to its first love: Fervency, zeal for God, and thirst for him as the deer pants for water. Loving what He loves and hating what He hates (when the body of Christ fulfils its mandate, the government will turn to us for Kingdom solutions, just as Joseph had the solutions to the seven-year famine).

The manifestation of the supernatural: Signs and wonders that will distinguish us from other faiths and turn the tide against idolatry and wickedness (for hospitals and care homes to empty as people are healed supernaturally; for education reforms, wholesome parenting and marriages, Kingdom businesses, etc.).

For the body of Christ to fulfil its mandate of advancing the Kingdom of God in every sphere of society.

Pastors and elders must have pliable hearts, teach the truth and the entire Gospel, and repent from falsehood and half-heartedness, not releasing congregations into their callings.

Our nation to become an apostolic nation, for Great Britain to align with its eternal destiny and purpose.

For the Prime Minster and her cabinet to have godly encounters like the apostle Paul did. For wisdom from Heaven to fulfil their mandates. For each one of them to have born-again spirits, including confidence, integrity, truth, humility, and honour.

For government and statutory officers' protection, preservation, work/life balance, and Kingdom strategies.

For Father God to bring order and alignment to the Labour Party so that they can sharpen and challenge our government to account in a positive way.

For those in the Labour Party in obscurity to be brought forward, and those with hardened hearts and wrong motives and agendas to be removed from office.

For the Lord to influence the negotiations of the Brexit.

Success with the Prime Minister's meetings with Germany, France, and Scotland.

Repentance for parents who are failures in bringing up their children in the way of the Lord.

Repentance in not adopting, fostering, mentoring, or befriending young people, resulting in government taking place of parents, and the rise of the gang culture, promiscuity, drug culture, abuse, etc.

Young people and families: Wholesomeness and true identities restored.

Truth, justice, and righteousness to be restored to every gate in society.

Protection from terrorist attacks.

For the body of Christ and Great Britain to be rightly aligned with Israel.

For the Prime Minister to forgive God and deal with undealt-with hurts from loss of her parents so that she will have no spiritual blinkers. For healing and deliverance from diabetes.

Restoration of finances.

Protection over Israel.

Jewish in Great Britain to receive salvation.

Lid taken off political correctness and replaced with righteousness, truth, and justice.

Restoration over all that was lost, and healing from every defilement from the prostitution of the EU.

*** Please see below Parliament statement of purpose. Declare daily over Parliament. Pray that this prayer is put into use again before each meeting. ***

Lord, the God of righteousness and truth, grant to our Queen and her government, to Members of Parliament and all in positions of responsibility, the guidance of your Spirit.

May they never lead the nation wrongly through love of power, desire to please, or unworthy ideals but laying aside all private interests and prejudices keep in mind their responsibility to seek to improve the condition of all mankind; so may your kingdom come and your name be hallowed. **Amen.**

Revelations:

Mr B shared a vision from the Lord, that, "the church was moving along a tramline back and forth in the same routine over and over again. It had become so mundane and stuck in its ways that it was unable to move along with the move of the Holy Spirit" (see Ezekiel 10).

Sword and flames: As our prayers go up, we put Angels of War to work on our behalf. As we declare His works, the Lord destroy the works of the enemy. The flames burn off the worthless and ignite flames of holiness and righteousness in believers.

As in Ezekiel, where the Lord is calling to the body of Christ to walk on water, to go deeper and further into the things of Him. It's time to see the fulfilment when the Earth sees the manifestation of the Son of God.

The Lord is cleaning the slate so that Great Britain is established on the right foundation. Just as He delivered the Israelites from Egypt to take them to the promised land, so has He delivered Great Britain from the EU for this country to occupy the place of promise (in the world) that the lord has planned for it.

Testimonies:

*** See link: http://blog.godreports.com/2012/01/for-child-art-prodigy-akiane-jesus-is-for-real/ ***

Catherine shared that her atheist sister returned to the Lord.

Scriptures:

- 1 Kings 11:11

- Daniel 9

- Psalms 24

- Psalms 85

- 1 Thessalonians 5:23-24

- Ezekiel 47:1-12

- Psalms 2

- Proverbs 3:5-8

- Proverbs 4.

Days 30 through 36: July 24 through 30, 2016:

I must say that this week's highlight for me has to be a great understanding of Father God's enduring love for the UK. His mercy and everlasting covenant will never leave us. You will see from this update that He is revealing things that are defiling the body of Christ and our nation so that we can repent, take authority, and release His truth, thereby enabling us all to live in freedom, wholesomeness, peace, and prosperity. And for truth, righteousness, and justice to be upheld, causing the advancement of Heaven on Earth. Praise Jesus!

Enjoy your read and please do register on Facebook here:

(https://www.facebook.com/events/631807060318106/)

If you haven't already done so for the 3-hour Acapella Praise & Worship on Saturday at 3 - 6 p.m., Parliament Square.

Thanks Giving:

Brexit means Brexit. The doors which the Lord shuts, no man can open, and the doors which He opens, no man can shut.

- It was reported that the USA will not discuss trade deals with the UK until its Brexit.

- The EU said that the UK must be prepared to accept all its laws to continue to access the single market, making it impossible for compromising Brexit.

- 2.5 million people who voted for the Labour Party during the last election said that they would vote for Theresa May in the next general election. This will eliminate the chances of a new government that would attempt to undermine Brexit.

- We'd been asking the Lord for keys, strategies, and revelations of legal demonic strongholds still in operation over the UK so that they could be renounced and the Lord would be given permission to enforce His healing over our nation.

  1. Julie Anderson of the Prayer Foundation and my spiritual mentor gave me "The 10-Point Plan," by Alice Bailey and the New World Order for the Destruction of Christianity" in the UK. as a tool to renounce curses spoken over our nation and to release blessings.

  2. Carol Baker gave me a folder detailing the ungodly laws that had been passed and other crucial information to help us war with precision.

- Full of praise and thanks for the Lord's hand of protection over the UK (in a previous update, you will recall that the Lord has placed a wall of fire over the UK and its Isles, not because we deserve it, but because He is a covenant-keeping God. Remember the rainbow over Parliament? It's the image we are using to promote the 3-Hour Worship & Praise event next Saturday. Please see here and register if you haven't already done so: https://www.facebook.com/events/631807060318106/).

Revelations:

- I saw a dam busted out with water that spread everywhere. Our prayers are about to cause a sudden turnaround.

- Margaret, a Jewish believer, saw lots of water swirling up the Big Ben tower. The Lord is about to restore our nation to its true identity and purpose.

- As we stood outside the Supreme Court rejecting ungodly laws over the land and replacing them with truth, plus asking the Lord to rend our economy (see 1 Kings 11:11), a huge number of motorcycle riders drove by with thundering noise. It felt that the actual ground was shaking. We knew then that the thundering sound was echoing the victory sound in the heavenly courts that was being released over the UK.

- Replacement theology in the body of Christ has given a false representation of Father God. He is a faith covenant-keeping, God. His love and mercy endures. He has not divorced Israel and replaced her with the Church. The church and redeemed Israel are His bride. The lie that Father God is a god who divorces has perpetuated the lie and deception that it's okay for believers to divorce their spouses whenever they choose to. This is a lie straight from the pits of Hell.

- A huge percentage of believers are spiritual orphans. Father God wants to restore their true identities and give them the revelation of who He really is and who we really are in Christ.

- The condition of the church today:

"And to the angel (divine messenger) of the church in [a]Pergamum write: These are the words of Him who has and wields the sharp two-edged sword [in judgment]: I know where you dwell, [a place] where Satan sits enthroned. Yet you are holding fast to My name, and you did not deny My faith even in the days of Antipas, My witness, My faithful one, who was killed (martyred) among you, where Satan dwells. But I have a few things against you, because you have there some [among you] who are holding to the [corrupt] teaching of Balaam, who taught Balak to put a stumbling block before the sons of Israel, [enticing them] to eat things that had been sacrificed to idols and to commit [acts of sexual] immorality. You also have some who in the same way are holding to the teaching of the Nicolaitans. Therefore repent [change your inner self—your old way of thinking, your sinful behaviour—seek God's will]; or else I am coming to you quickly, and I will make war and fight against them with the sword of My mouth [in judgment]. He who has an ear, let him hear and heed what the Spirit says to the churches. To him who overcomes [the world through believing that Jesus is the Son of God], to him I will give [the privilege of eating] some of the hidden manna, and I will give him a white stone with a new name engraved on the stone which no one knows except the one who receives it" Revelation 2:12-17 (Amplified).

- The function of the church is to advance God's Kingdom in every gate of society. Many believers are earning a living rather than fulfilling their godly destiny callings (e.g., for mental health problems, there are believers assigned with Kingdom solutions to bring about healing and restorations; for the elderly in care homes, there are believers with Kingdom solutions so that the elderly will no longer require this. Cancer -- There are believers with innovations to cure cancer and supernatural powers to deliver through laying on of hands, etc. It's time for the body of Christ to awaken from the mundane, luke-warmness and deception and lay hold of their true identities and callings in advancing the Lord's calling for the UK (Earth is crying out for the manifestations of the Son of God).

Declarations:

- Mercy over the EU nations (particularly France and Germany). Hearts turned to God in repentance so that He can heal their land.

- Thank You, Lord, for the call of the UK as an apostolic nation. We are called out of the EU to lead others.

- The sword of the Lord cut off and deal with all the principalities working against the UK.

- We declare that signs and wonders manifest in the body of Christ, provoking jealousy from non-believers and causing them to desire Christ, exposing that other religions are dead.

- Father God, mend our economy (see 1 Kings 11:11).

- Spiritual watchmen on the wall in every church and gate in society, be alert and ready, not giving place to weariness.

- Father God, bless our security, including police, secret service, and people in positions of authority with Kingdom strategies, wisdom, and discernment.

- Station angels around the MI6, police, etc.

- Father God, trouble our Cabinet officers in the night like King Nebuchadnezzar if you must in order that they are humbled and pliable in advancing Your Kingdom agenda in every gate of society (i.e., truth, righteousness, and justice). Lawlessness and deception have no place.

- Intelligence with Israel stronger. Balfour Treaty fulfilled.

- Healing and deliverance to our Prime Minister, who has diabetes. Her parents died prematurely, so she may have unresolved issues with Father God. We declare encounters like those that Paul and Moses had so that the PM has a born-again spirit.

- Father God, bring strong conviction upon the twenty-six Bishops in the House of Lords. Let their hearts come ablaze for you and have encounters like Moses had. Give them spirits like Daniel, who refused to compromise truth or yield to the fear of man, love of position, power, or money. If their hearts are not pliable, then replace with Kingdom-minded Bishops who will stand for integrity and truth. Renounce and reject every ungodly law.

- Revive the 1661 Prayer in the House of Parliament.

- The body of Christ lay hold of the old wells and mantles (e.g., William Wilberforce, Shaftesbury, John G. Lake, Wigglesworth, etc.).

- Heal broken families.

- May the fragrance of Jesus be upon every believer.

To the praise of His glory following Great Britain's decision to Brexit from the EU, we not only successfully had forty days of intercession at Parliament Square to reinforce the victory that the Lord had given the United Kingdom, but also during this period, some of the things listed below unfolded:

- The Lord helped appoint a new Prime Minister who is a Christian and a church goer.

- New Cabinet Office.

- The Prime Minister said Brexit means Brexit. The USA won't have trade discussions until Article 50 is imposed. The EU won't give access to single market unless we adhere to all their laws.

- A shake-up in the Labour and UKIP Parties so that there is proper alignment with Father God's plans for our nation.

- Thwarted terrorist plans.

- Countries outside of the EU want to trade with the EU.

- The need for stability in the economy.

- Justice brought to light through the Chilcot Report.

- Awakening of intercessors across the nation.

- The Lord said He wants to heal our land, but the body of Christ must first return to Him as our first love.

- Call to awakening of the body of Christ to supernatural living, thus displaying the Lord's glory)

- Call for the true revelation of Father God and identities as children of God, as well as an intimacy and true worship with Father God.

- Call to align Kingdom assignments, deployment, and discipleship.

- Call to align with Israel and break off of every ungodly alliance, including the spirit of Islam.

- Stirring up a desire for God's Kingdom to be advanced in every sphere of society.

- Ripe harvest; People are looking for answers and solutions to life.

Days 37 through 40: August 1 through 3, 2016:

On the fortieth day of prayer, Miss M, one of the intercessors, got this revelation: "As I was going to the prayer session, I was just singing quietly in my spirit and humming the song, 'In Christ Alone', when I had a vision of doves flying over Parliament Square. It happened three times. The dove, as we know, is symbolic of the Holy Spirit. God is saying that He is bringing His order to bear upon our government. Even as the Holy Spirit hovered over the face of the Earth at creation, I believe that the Lord is going to bring order out of the chaos that we are currently experiencing as a nation."

The Lord's been impressing this Scripture on my heart:

"He said, 'Open the window toward the east', and he opened it. Then Elisha said, 'Shoot'! And he shot. And he said, 'The LORD'S arrow of victory, even the arrow of victory over Aram; for you will defeat the Arameans at Aphek until you have destroyed them'. Then he said, 'Take the arrows', and he took them. And he said to the king of Israel, 'Strike the ground', and he struck it three times and stopped. So the man of God was angry with him and said, 'You should have struck five or six times, then you would have struck Aram until you would have destroyed it. But now you shall strike Aram only three times" 2 Kings 13:17-19 (Amplified).

As watchmen, we cannot afford to go weary or lose momentum in our intercession. We must continue to pray until we see the Lord's Kingdom manifest in our nation. MPs may be on vacation, but the devil is not! Therefore, we continue to meet at Parliament Square on Sundays at 5:00 p.m. to intercede for the UK.

Please pray on the key points of prayer given below, which we were led to pray about today:

- Intimacy with God, to replace the spirit of religion, complacency, compromise, performance-led lives, idolatry, greed, love of power and money across the body of Christ, the government, and the UK.

- Restoration of Families: The emphasis today was on families. The Lord is going to start dealing with the orphan spirit plaguing individuals and families. He will not only restore true identities, but also raise up fathers and mothers to mentor, coach, counsel, foster, adopt, or befriend the orphan (spiritual and in the natural); also, the restoration of broken marriages.

- The body of Christ must have Kingdom-oriented discipleship programs, and sound teaching on sacred sex, parenting, young people, and marriage.

- Holiday season: Parents and the body of Christ invest quality time with children. Cabinet and government members have encounters with the Lord, just as King

Nebuchadnezzar did, and humbly acquire strategies and wisdom from the Lord as they seek Him for direction for blueprints for policies and legislation to lead our nation forward to its heavenly calling.

- Order and alignment into the Labour Party.

- Restoration of godly laws: Truth, justice, and righteousness to replace ungodly laws passed through Parliament.

- Balfour Treaty: The government and the Queen to fulfil the treaty. Reconciliation with and a visit to Israel.

- St Margaret's and Westminster Abbey be filled with the presence of the Lord, Spirit-filled ministers, five-fold ministry in operation. Healing and deliverance ministry, Kingdom teaching, Spirit-filled worship and prayer meetings held there, discipleship programs, prophetic sessions, and counselling. Open Heaven where MPs get to meet with God and tourists meet with God. Beacon of light that dispels darkness in Parliament.

- Churches come alive to Jesus. Believers realise their true identities, alignment with God as Father and step into their kingdom callings at every gate of society.

- The Lord reigns over the UK. His mercy prevails over judgement and as we continue to seek his face and follow his leading we will see him manifest his glory over us and our nation. Those who do not know him will desire him and come to the light.

Thank you for your love and support. Together we advance His Kingdom.

May the Lord bless and continue to perfect everything that concerns you. And may you fulfil the love story that Father God has written concerning your life in Christ Jesus' Name.

We ended the forty-day prayer with three hours of praise and worship at Parliament Square on Saturday, August 6, 2016, as that was the earliest date available to secure a booking with the GLA and the Lord gave us a vision of the ground-breaking up like an earthquake and lots of water started to gush out and spread outward from Parliament Square. The Holy Spirit is about to move over our nation. Ungodly foundations will be shaken out and replaced with godly foundations. There will be a restoration of morality and goodness in our society. Secularism and idolatry will be shaken out of their places, as unprecedented numbers of people turn their hearts to Christ Jesus.

NEXT STEPS

During darkness, light shines brightest (see John 1:5). Our 40 Days Prayer Assignment is just the beginning of many more prayer initiatives that the Lord is mobilising across Great Britain to create a prayer movement that will be the catalyst for social reformation and revival that's about to manifest in our nation, thereby displacing wickedness, idolatry, brokenness, fear, hatred, confusion, frustrations, poverty and disharmony, etc.

- The Holy Spirit has started to ignite the hearts of many more faceless believers to take the Lord's Kingdom authority and pray until something happens in every area and gate of society.

The question is, will you be a part of the prayer movement or will it be business as usual for you?

Prayer meetings and walks are about to take place at every gate of society (i.e. in homes, schools, universities, workplaces, and communities). We truly are in the days when the army of the Lord is rising.

"and if My people, who are called by My Name, humble themselves, and pray and seek (crave, require as a necessity) My face and turn from their wicked ways, then I will hear [them] from heaven, and forgive their sin and heal their land." 2 Chronicles 7:14 (Amplified)

Printed in the United States
By Bookmasters